There are 135 interconnected short stories in this book. Some are hilarious, some quite serious, many are great fun and upbeat while others are really sad. Your emotions will go up and down like a roller coaster, but in the process, that ride will be well worth it as you will be thoroughly entertained.

There are tales of childhood mischief, adventure, hot rods, romance, suspense, parenting, business advice, the newspaper industry, history, heartbreak, a puppy and even slot machines!

Most of the stories occur in and around Minneapolis/St. Paul, Minnesota, Birmingham, Alabama and Omaha, Nebraska. If you are familiar with any of these cities, you'll instantly recognize the locales mentioned.

Interestingly, each and every name in this book is real with one exception, and that one was changed due to a most unsavory deed perpetrated by that individual. That story will make your blood boil.

Buckle up for a crazy Baby Boomer ride. You'll laugh, you'll cry, but most of all, you'll fall in love with RAMBLINGS.

Ramblings

of a Baby Boomer wannabe

Tom Golden

ISBN 978-1-64559-319-5 (Paperback)
ISBN 978-1-64559-320-1 (Digital)

Covenant Books, Inc.
11661 Hwy 707
Murrells Inlet, SC 29576
www.covenantbooks.com

*I dedicate this book to
my big brother Jerry.*

Preface

I did not have any intention of writing a book. It happened strictly by accident. I was simply jotting down some of my memories and got carried away. Now that it's actually a book, I have high hopes that somebody out there will read it. I wrote far more than I had ever anticipated or intended; and did so over a period of about three years. I'd work on it for a while, then walk away and leave it—sometimes for months at a time. That may have been a good thing as each time I returned to it, I'd re-read what I had written and then try to make improvements. I revised the book nine times before finally submitting it to a publisher. Then, shortly after sending it off, I did draft number 10.

I never did use an outline—I just let the memories flow. I found it amazing how one led right into another. I had to divide the memories into timelines which became chapters. I saved each chapter individually on my computer so I could quickly access a time period to add another story. Sometimes I'd get stuck on a name that I hadn't thought of in many, many years. Trying to concentrate and force it out never seemed to work.

What did produce a result was simply leaving the keyboard and doing something else. My brain, apparently no longer feeling any obligation to recall the name, would just cough it up while I was out cutting the grass, watching TV or buying Twinkies at the gas station. I had to keep pen and paper handy to jot down names, story ideas and funny quips before they vanished.

As I reflected on what I had written, I thought about the various individuals who had been involved in my stories. I wondered how each might feel reading about themselves? The facts are the facts (as I remember them), but my intention was never to hurt, anger, humiliate or embarrass any one. I recognize that their memories of the events described in this book may differ from mine … let's face it, time and age can certainly alter our recollections. Please know that I wrote this book with the intent of being totally honest, sincere and forthright. Both my publisher and I regret any unintentional harm resulting from the publishing and marketing of RAMBLINGS of a Baby Boomer wannabe.

Writing it was a wonderful experience. It allowed me to re-live many events of long ago. Some made me laugh out loud, others made me cry. But, I got it all out—well, most of it anyway. For me, the journey was worthwhile and therapeutic … I hope it is somewhat entertaining for you.

Thanks for taking the time to read my ramblings. I think you'll get a few laughs … and you might even shed a tear or two.

Tom Golden

Chapter 1

Chapter 1

A Little about My Ancestry

I've always thought of myself as a Baby Boomer, but technically, I may not be. As we all know, Baby Boomers were born after WWII. The widely accepted BB generation's range in dates is 1946–1964. The war in Europe ended when Germany surrendered on May 8, 1945. The war in the Pacific ended when Japan surrendered on August 15, 1945. BUT, President Truman didn't declare the "hostilities at an end" until December 31, 1945. I'm not sure what caused the lag time…possibly holiday shopping.

I was born on May 24, 1945, in St. Paul, Minnesota. That was clearly AFTER the war with Germany ended but BEFORE the war with Japan ended. So, as it turns out, I might be a dangling part of the tail end of the Silent Generation…the same generation as my older brother. Well, I OBJECT! You see, the start and end dates of the Silent Generation and the Baby Boomer Generation depend on the source you use. Some say the Silent Generation was from the mid-1920s to the **early**-1940s. Yet others the mid-1920's to the **mid**-1940s. I'll give them this, they all pretty much agree on when it started, just not when it ended. Obviously, that impacts when the Baby Boomer Generation actually began. So, as long as there is a little wiggle room, I'm going to claim to be a Baby Boomer. Stick that in your pipe and smoke it! Now there's a phrase you don't hear much anymore…or if you do, it tends to be more literal.

My father was half Irish and half German and my mother was 100 percent German. My paternal great-grandfather emigrated from Mayo, Ireland, and initially lived in the New York City area. His son, my paternal grandfather, John Henry Golden, was born in Hackensack, New Jersey. I remember him as short, maybe five feet seven inches, old, retired (from a career as a cloth buyer/inspector for men's suits), somewhat overweight, and totally bald. Now I readily admit that at one point he may have been younger, taller, carried less weight, and had hair. I've no actual evidence, however, to substantiate that.

The story, as I heard it, was that he ended up in Minnesota strictly by accident. He had had serious respiratory problems as a young man, and his doctor advised that he consider moving to a drier climate. He bought a ticket and boarded a train bound for Phoenix. Maybe if he had just quit puffing on cigars all the time he could have saved himself a trip. But, be that as it may, the train made a stop at the downtown St. Paul depot. As Grandpa wandered around the cavernous building, he came upon a lovely, very tall, and slender young woman…a Ms. Gertrude Emma Rosalia Wagner. I'm not exactly sure what happened after that initial meeting—but I do know that Grandpa never re-boarded the train and Ms. Wagner became Grandma. They were somewhat of an odd pairing—he short and stout, she tall and lean. Do you remember Boris and Natacha from *Rocky and Bullwinkle*? There you go.

Grandma & Grampa Golden

Me and Grampa Golden on his apartment steps 1947 or 1948

My maternal grandmother, Catherine A. (Schroeder) Newman, passaged all alone from Bavaria on a ship bound for the New World when she was just twenty-one. The year was 1911. I have no idea why she came to the USA by herself. I do recall something about her having a cousin in Minnesota, so that was her destination. I'm guessing that after arriving in Minnesota she lived with that cousin. She spoke German and very broken English when she arrived but was able to read and write both. She became a cleaning lady for the wealthy families who lived in the big mansions on Summit Ave. in St. Paul.

At some point she met my maternal grandfather, Alexander (Al) Newman. He and his brother Mux were born in Minnesota after their parents had emigrated from Germany in the 1880s. Their last name was actually Neumann, but because of poor penmanship, the immigration officer was unable to read what had been written, so he asked, "Last name?" The reply, "Neumann," was written down as "Newman." Grandpa grew up on a farm in Stillwater, Minnesota, an old logging town on the St. Croix River, east of St. Paul. The St. Croix separates Minnesota and the *Viking* fans from Wisconsin and the *Packer* fans. Both states, however, have this in common…brandy consumption (winter antifreeze).

Grandma & Grampa Newman

Grandpa Al was a large, powerfully built man. He had worked at Schmidt Brewery on Seventh Street in St. Paul in the loading dock area. Because neither grandparent ever drove a car, he walked the ten blocks to and from work each day regardless of weather conditions. *(Imagine doing that for forty years!)* Even at an advancing age, his arms were still unbelievably strong from many years of lifting cases and barrels of beer. I remember once in their small house on the corner of Duke and Banfil Streets, he demonstrated his strength for me in two ways: first by tearing a phone book in half and secondly by lifting a dining room chair with one hand wrapped around the bottom of one leg. The chair came up EVENLY. Try it.

Mom and Dad

My mother's name was Helen Alberta (Newman) Golden. She was born in St. Paul in 1914 and grew up with her brother, Albert, eight years her junior. She attended Mechanic Arts High School, which once stood near the state capital building in St. Paul. Upon graduation in 1932, she went to work for Northwestern Bell Telephone on Dale St. near Selby Ave. She was very attractive at five feet five inches, blue eyes, brown hair, and a nice figure. She was also quite athletic, musically inclined (played piano), and very outgoing. And how she loved having fun.

She grew up speaking English and German, and I recall her reverting to German when she got angry. I think it was her way of swearing in front of me and my brother without us knowing it (*but we knew*).

In 1940 Mom and Dad married—both were twenty-six. When she got pregnant, she quit the phone company job to become a full-time homemaker. Years later, when older brother Jerry and I were in high school, she took a job as a switchboard operator at the Minnesota State Capital Building. Remember Ernestine from *Laugh-In*... "That's one ringy-dingy"? Well, that was her job.

Dad, John Richard Golden, was also born in St. Paul in 1914. He had three sisters: Gertrude, Helen, and Marion. At age fourteen, he lied about his age and got a job at the St. Paul Main Post Office working in the Special Delivery department. That meant that he drove, with no license, to hand deliver letters and packages. He was required to get a signature for each. He too graduated in 1932 but from Cretin High School...a Christian Brother's all-boys institute with a mandatory US Army ROTC program.

He was tall and lean at six feet two inches and 180, athletic, and he had a great sense of humor. *Example:* when still in high school, he and his dad (Grandpa Golden), were out for a walk one hot summer evening when Dad spotted a buddy park his car and walk across University Ave. and into White Castle. They stole his car—well, only kind of. They pushed it down the street and around the corner, then watched as he came out with a bag of burgers and crossed the street. Dad swore the guy actually reached around in the air where the car had been parked as if it may have become invisible while he was in buying sliders.

After graduating and leaving the post office, he became a motorcycle cop patrolling a military complex in Rosemount, Minnesota. It housed the Gopher Ordnance Works (a munitions plant run by Dupont) that employed twenty thousand workers during WW II. After that he was a bowling alley manager and then a partner in a beer joint... Connie & Jack's Tavern. That was a lot of fun, but also a lot of hours for very little money. He was now married with two kids, so it was time to get serious about a long-term career.

He was offered a job at a calendar and playing card printing company called Brown & Bigelow. He operated a machine and earned all of seventy-five cents an hour—but B & B would become his career. The company was growing and adding new "remembrance advertising" products, so he felt that there was a lot of opportunity for advancement. He went to night school at the University of Minnesota and used that education, coupled with his drive and ambition, to move ahead. He became the general manager of their East Hennepin production plant in Minneapolis and was later named vice president of manufacturing for the entire company. He then became president of a subsidiary company called Quality Park Box & Envelope. He'd grin and ask Mom, "How does it feel to sleep with the president?" She'd always respond, "Just like the first lady." He loved that job despite having to travel frequently to their other facilities around the country. Then after a couple of years, he was asked to re-join the parent firm as VP/general manager. He retired in 1979.

Mom and Dad met at a bar on Wabasha St. in downtown St. Paul in the late thirties. He was there with his best friend, Mike Wagner (no relation to my grandmother), and she was with a girl-friend from work. The four of them struck up a conversation, had a couple of drinks, and danced. Now I should mention that Mom was engaged at the time to a guy studying to be a pharmacist. She once told me that compared to Dad, her fiancé was a "fuddy-duddy" (meaning rather dull). He always needed to go home to study when she wanted to go out and have some fun. Well, our soon-to-be dad was now supplying the fun, so the engagement to the medicine man was soon broken off. I'll say this, the folks did know how to party!

Mom and Dad, October 5, 1940

They married on October 5, 1940. Their love, their devotion to each other, and their marriage, lasted for seventy-two years. Isn't that remarkable? Dad died in 2012 at age ninety-eight. Mom died three years later at one hundred one.

Como Park

I grew up in an area of St. Paul called Como Park. It is just a couple of miles northwest of downtown. The area consists not only of typical older homes, but also a huge park. It used to be a city park, but now it's considered a regional park. There is a lake with a large lakeside pavilion, a zoo, an eighteen-hole golf course, and a beautifully lit fountain. Midway up a hill overlooking the fountain stands the decorative and flower-laden Gates Ajar. In addition, Como has plenty of open parkland and forested areas, picnic pavilions, tennis courts, walking trails, a waterfall cascading into a pond that contains a giant concrete frog, a community swimming pool, numerous baseball and softball fields, a huge glass-enclosed Victorian tropical garden conservatory, and an amusement park (mostly kiddie rides). A large bronze statue of Friedrich von Shiller stands at the divide of two park roads. He was a famous German writer who fought for the expression of free speech and the equal rights of all. The statue was commissioned and erected by German immigrants in the early 1900s to honor their German heritage and the ideals of their new home.

I may have missed a few things, but you get my point, it was a pretty nice *place* to grow up. And, the mid-fifties and early-sixties were also a great *time* to grow up. They were truly *HAPPY DAYS*.

Home Sweet Home

The first house that I remember was at 998 Como Place. It was a small older home with a finished attic, and it sat on a postage-stamp-size corner lot. The little freestanding one-car garage took up most of the backyard. But there was room for the clothes poles and the clothes lines. EVERYBODY had clothes lines. The main floor of the house consisted of a small enclosed front porch, a living room, dining room, tiny kitchen, and two bedrooms with a bathroom in between (the only bathroom in the house). A door in the dining room opened to steep steps leading to the attic bedroom that I shared with my older brother, Jerry. (*When I was very little, I guess I had trouble pronouncing Js and Rs so I called Jerry… GO-GEE*).

998 Como Place, St. Paul, MN

Sugar Rush

Back then, kids were allowed to run around the neighborhood unattended without fear of them being snatched up by perverts. That being the case, the kids knew everybody within a couple block radius of their house and everybody knew whose kids were whose. Most moms were home during the day while their husbands were off at work. They not only watched out for their own kids, but every kid in the neighborhood. At about age five, I was actually out knocking on doors asking each mom who answered for a cookie. I almost always got one too. On one such excursion, I was surprised to see a husky middle-aged man answer the door. A man at home during the day was pretty darn unusual. But what scared me was that he was wearing a gun in a shoulder holster. Despite some fear, I went ahead and made my request. He smiled and invited me in. He disappeared into the kitchen and then came back with a cookie. We sat in his living room, and he asked me my name and where I lived. I asked him if his wife was home, and he told me that he lived alone. That was also unusual as far as I was concerned. Then I got up the courage to ask about the gun. He explained that he was a St. Paul police detective and was just getting ready to leave for his shift. He was a very nice man, and he became a regular stop on my cookie quests.

It was 1950, and I recall bottled milk being placed on our back porch steps and Joe, the mailman, stopping each day to chat with me. I'd frequently walk along with him going from house to house as he delivered the mail. We'd talk the whole time. On occasion Joe would reach into his mailbag; pull out a candy bar; and hand it to me, saying, "Don't tell your mom." He was such a happy-go-lucky guy. You know, back then people were kind, friendly, trusting, and they never seemed to be in a big hurry. They always took the time to be civil and to talk—even to kids. As the years passed, and I began attending school, I didn't see Joe much during the school year but I did see him nearly every day over the summer months.

Here's an odd memory... I recall a horse-drawn wagon going by our house weekly with the driver hollering, "RAGS." I loved the "clip-clop" sound that the horse's hoofs made on the pavement. I could hear the man yelling, "RAGS," even after he was long out of sight. I've read that rag men purchased rags, newspapers, metal, etc. They were truly ahead of their time—they were recyclers!

Peace and Quiet

Just a block down from our house, running eleven blocks along the south side of Front Street, was a huge Catholic cemetery called Calvary. I loved to ride my bike in there, not because I was obsessed with death or anything, but because it had nice hilly tree-lined roads and no traffic. I'd always smile and wave at the cemetery workers (grounds keepers and grave diggers) as I rode by. They most always smiled and waved back. I never found the cemetery to be a sad or depressing place, maybe because I was just a kid. I didn't have much of a grip on what death was. But I soon found out.

The cemetery caretaker's son, Ron Bierbaum, was a couple of years older than me; and like most kids in the area, he was a student at St. Andrew's. They lived just across the street from the cemetery, and their house sat on a large corner lot. Adjacent to the house was a large barn-like outbuilding where cemetery equipment was stored. I'd occasionally ride my bike over that way just to say hi to him. He was always nice to me, but because he was a couple of years older, we were never good friends. Age made a difference. Across the street from Ron's house, on the other corner, was Howard Monument Company. They made and inscribed nearly all the headstones that went into Calvary. Most were made from granite, but there were some marble ones too. I learned that marble didn't hold up to the elements nearly as well as granite, but some people insisted on having it. For some reason, when I was about seven, I began hanging out around that monument company much to the chagrin of the owners and workers. I constantly got shooed out of the place with threats of "We're going to call your folks." I, however, just couldn't seem to stay away; and they eventually allowed me to watch them work. My persistence had paid off, and this was a very important life lesson for me as you'll see later on. My parents eventually became aware of my somewhat unusual hangout. Dad went down and talked to the owner, who assured him that they'd watch out for me so that I didn't get hurt. I'm sure my parents wondered if I was going to grow up to be a tombstone engraver.

Belly Up to the Bar

Next door to that business was an old house that had been converted into a working man's neighborhood saloon. I think it was just beer and short-order food (no booze unless you brought your own in). The Pitzel family owned it, and they lived upstairs of the business. Their son Dick and I became friends, and he led me into my first beer joint—at age seven. Before it opened for business, we were allowed to sit at the bar and his dad would give us glasses of pop (the

Minnesota term for soda or soft drink). I vividly recall the smell of beer and stale cigarette smoke in that place, and I didn't care much for it. I stopped going in even though it meant giving up the FREE pop. I don't think that my parents ever knew about me bellying up to the bar at such a tender age.

Nuts

Our house had a small enclosed back porch with steps leading to the back yard. Jerry and I had been feeding a squirrel with walnuts that Mom kept on hand to make chocolate chip cookies. We had named the rodent Junior. I'm not sure why. We kept coaxing the little bugger closer and closer with each passing day. Eventually it began eating the nuts right out of our hands, and we were ecstatic. While very tame, it was still a wild animal as I learned the hard way. One day I was feeding it, and I must have moved too quickly…it bit me. Thankfully, it didn't have rabies! Good thing as neither of us bothered to tell the folks about the incident.

Medic

While living on Como Place, Jerry sent me to the hospital numerous times. Once we were playing cowboys, and he tied my hands and feet. I guess I was the bad guy! We were in the dining room, and he made me sit down on the floor—then, for some reason, he pushed me…and pushed me hard. The back of my head hit the metal radiator. I got my very first stitches…and scar number 1 at Children's Hospital.

Sometime later, we were once again playing cowboys in our bedroom. I'll be damned if I wasn't tied up again! Standing there with hands and feet bound, I guess he just couldn't resist the temptation to push me. I lost my balance and fell to the floor, landing chin first on the corner of a partially opened bottom dresser drawer. Back to Children's Hospital and Dr. Steinberg for more stitches…and scar number 2. Those painful experiences may be the reasons that I never really cared for Western movies.

Then, one winter day, we were out climbing around the hole that had been dug for the foundation of a new home. It was only about a block from our house. There was a blanket of wet heavy snow on the ground, making it perfect for building a snowman OR, better yet, having a snowball fight. Snowballs flew back and forth, and all was going well until Jerry made a snowball containing a pretty good-sized rock. He later claimed it was unintentional—I still remain unconvinced. He pegged it with deadly accuracy, and it nailed me right in the back of the head. Yup, more stitches…and scar number 3. By now we were all on a first name basis with the doctors and personnel at Children's.

Craftsman

Kitty-corner (some say Catty-corner) was the Nichol's residence. It was a small square box of a house with red shutters, a red shingle roof, and white wooden siding. They were, however, the envy of the neighborhood because they had a new DOUBLE garage. That was almost unheard of in the early fifties. I don't really remember much about Mr. Nichol's except that he drove a Nash from the automotive division of the Nash-Kelvinator Corporation. Yes, Kelvinator, the refrigerator people. I suspect that it was the same design team for both product lines. What an ugly damn car. To make matters worse, it was turquoise. Anyway, they had a niece about my age who would come to visit for a few weeks each summer. She lived in Davenport, Iowa. *Useless historical note: at one-time sofas were called davenports.* So this girl's name was Vickie Music. Isn't that a great name? Vickie Music. We'd spend a lot of time together on her visits. I had a crush on her, but sadly, I was already married (but that's another story). So one day she and I were hanging out in that new double garage when I noticed all the great tools mounted on the pegboard. I decided right then and there to impress Vickie by demonstrating how well I could use them. I took down a sharp-edged chisel and a hammer and proceeded to take big V-shaped chunks of wood out of the front board of the new workbench. I was quite thorough and made sure that I did all three exposed sides. I was pretty proud of my notching abilities until Mr. Nichols pulled his ugly turquoise Nash into the driveway. I had heard some swear words in my young life, but not at this volume—and not directed at me. While I can't recall if Vickie had been impressed or not, I can remember that my father paid Mr. Nichols for some new workbench boards and I ended up with a sore rear end.

Enough

Jerry, being three and a half years older, was considerably bigger than me. Fights with him never ended well for yours truly. He'd pin me down, kneel over me with one hand on each of my shoulders, then let spit drip onto my face. One day, however, I got sweet revenge. We were down the block in a neighbor's back yard with some other kids when he began taunting me. He kept it up and kept it up until I was really furious. There just happened to be a four-foot piece of two-by-four lying on the ground. I suspect that it was a gift from God. I picked it up and let him have it—right in the head. Now it was his turn to get stitches—AND a tetanus shot as the board had a rusty bent nail in it. Our poor parents.

School

Nearly everyone in the neighborhood was Catholic and belonged to St. Andrew's Church. Most of the kids went to St. Andrew's school (grades one through eight) including Jerry and me. There were no school busses, and Dad left early taking our only car, so Jerry and I walked a little over half mile to and from school each day. Mom actually believed that because we both left at the same time that we walked to school together. HA. About a block away from the house Jerry would "ditch" me, and I'd often end up walking alone. But I was a pretty happy and good-natured kid, so it never bothered me. During the day, Mom had only the street car, or maybe a neighbor with a car, for transportation. But you know, somehow it all worked out. People actually walked to the neighborhood grocery stores back then, so we all survived.

St. Andrew's was run by the Sisters of Notre Dame. They were strict and demanding. There would be no fooling around in their classrooms…period. If you are not Catholic, maybe you thought that the stories about kids getting their knuckles smacked with a ruler was just fantasy. I'm here to tell you that it was most certainly not fantasy when you were on the receiving end. I always wanted to be the funny kid in class, so my knuckles were constantly sore. And let me be clear about this—there was no court of appeal. You could go home and tell your parents that your teacher hit you for no reason at all, and the reply would always be: "Good. I'm sure you had it coming." Pleading your case did absolutely no good. The nuns were ALWAYS right, and you were always WRONG. More about St. Andrew's later.

Lemonade

One summer day Jerry and I had a lemonade stand set up down on Front St. across from the cemetery. It was a pretty busy road, so we thought that we could make a little money. A car pulled up across from us, parked, and a man wearing a suit and a hat got out. He crossed over, and we were ready to pour him a glass of ice cold lemonade, but as it turned out, he had something else in mind. He wanted to promote our little venture by putting our picture in the *St. Paul Dispatch*. He was a newspaper photographer, and I guess we were one of those human-interest stories.

First, he needed to stage it just right. He wanted me to move across to the cemetery side of the street and then point back over at Jerry who was sitting at the table. I refused because I was afraid of being in front of his car. To my way of thinking, it could suddenly come to life and run me over. The photographer laughed, showed me that he had the keys, and assured me that the car could not possibly move without them. Well, I looked over and observed that the street was perfectly level. I guess if it couldn't start without the keys and it couldn't roll because it was on level ground, then maybe, just maybe, it would be safe. But one last thing—Mom and Dad had told me that I had to be VERY careful on Front Street because some cars drove too fast. So I reluctantly agreed to move providing he walked me over there and then came back to get me after he had taken the picture. He quickly agreed. So there I was, sitting in a chair, pointing, but nervously glancing sideways, at that parked car—just in case. Before leaving, he did buy a glass of lemonade, and the picture appeared the very next day on the front page of the "Metro" section.

They Get 'Em Both Ways

The Golden brothers get 'em coming and going on Front street. While big brother Jerry, 10, dispenses his thirst quenchers on the far side of street, his junior partner, Thomas, 7, points out the oasis to motorists on the south of the street. Business is good, beamed Jerry. "Twenty-four cents so far," he grinned. They live at 998 Como place.—Staff Photo.

Hitched

Okay, before I forget—my first marriage. One of my dad's best friends was Connie Bettendorf. They fished together, played ball together, and, at one point, even owned a bar together—Connie & Jack's. Well, Connie and his wife Marie lived only a block away, and they often socialized with our parents—sometimes at our house, sometimes at their house. Most often the kids were dragged along.

They had four children—Jim, Jeanne, Sharon, and Maggie. Like all the other kids, they also attended St. Andrew's. Sharon was a year or two younger than me, but we always ended up together on various outings and trips. One day her older brother Jim said that because we were together so much, we should probably get married. So be it. She wore a white dress. I wore a white shirt and my St. Andrew's uniform blue tie. Jim dressed in black like a priest. The wedding was in the Bettendorf back yard under a grape vine-covered arbor. I believe Jim used an actual prayer book, or I guess, it could have been a stolen hymnal. I can't recall who was there, but I do know that no parents had been invited to the ceremony. Jim insisted that we kiss after pronouncing us man and wife and that was my very first lip-to-lip kiss.

Eventually our parents found out about the wedding and were appropriately amused. Some weeks later her family and ours were staying in a lake cabin. I have no idea what lake—Minnesota has over ten thousand of them *(thus, the license plate slogan "Land of 10,000 Lakes")*. It was getting late and the parents, who were sitting at the kitchen table playing cards, told us kids to go to bed. That's when I, as an innocent seven-year-old, asked, "Is it okay if I sleep with Sharon?" At first there was stunned silence, then an explosion of laughter from our parents so loud I think it was heard on the other side of the lake. So much for our honeymoon.

Me, Dad & Jerry, 1952

The End of Innocence

When I was eight, I overheard my mother telling somebody on the telephone that Joe, our nice mailman, had suddenly died of a heart attack. I just ran up to my room and broke into tears. I had never lost a friend or a relative before. I learned that Joe's funeral would be at St. Andrew's Church, which was just a block away from the school. I asked my mother if I could attend, but she said no—probably thinking that it would be too intense for a child. If that is what she had been thinking, she was right.

I'd always been an obedient child, but decided right then and there that I was going to ignore my mother's wishes. The morning of Joe's funeral I skipped out of school between classes and walked over to the church. I immediately saw the casket draped in a fancy cloth up in the front. I knew my friend Joe, our mailman, was in there. I sat in a back pew watching, listening, and sobbing. A nun had seen me leave school and walk across the back parking lot. She called my mother to report me missing. Mom knew immediately where I had gone. "Check the funeral going on at the church," she said. A retired nun from the convent was sent over to find me and bring me back to class. I glanced up at the elderly sister as she stood in the aisle looking at me. She could see the tears streaming down my cheeks. Instead of dragging me back to school, she genuflected (well, kind of a half genuflection), slid into the pew beside me, sat down, and never uttered a single word. She had found me, but she had no intention of disturbing me in this time of grief. Chalk one up for the sisters. My mother never said a word to me about disobeying her.

After that funeral, Calvary Cemetery took on a whole new meaning. My friend Joe was now buried there, and it had become a place of sadness for me. I never again rode my bike on those tree-lined roads.

New Digs

In June 1955 we moved from Como Place into a brand-new house just constructed on one of the last remaining lots in the entire

Como area. The address was 1263 Osage Street, and it was about two blocks from the lake. While only a mile from our old house, it felt like we had moved to a totally different world. The homes were newer, many larger, all had much bigger yards; and it just felt more suburban despite still being in the city. I was only ten, and while I loved the house, I missed my friends. I'd ride my bike over to the "old" neighborhood for visits, but that ended as I made friends around our new house. I had no idea what "Osage" meant back then, but now assume it may have referred to the Osage Indian Tribes. But even that seems odd as I don't think that the Osage Indians were ever in Minnesota—let alone Como Park.

1263 Osage Street, St. Paul, MN

The house was a rambler (what we called single-story ranch-style houses) with an attached single-car garage, a stacked stone facade, and a large picture window in the living room. It was designed as a three-bedroom, one-bath house, but before the construction had been completed, our folks decided to keep the wall open between the living room and the front bedroom so it could be used as a combination den (now called a home office) and TV room. Jerry and I continued to share a bedroom.

On a square footage basis, the new house wasn't much bigger than the old house. Some of the rooms, however, were considerably larger. The kitchen was twice the size as was the living room with its beautiful stone fireplace. The dining room was smaller, and our bedroom was a fraction the size of our old attic bedroom. There was still just one bathroom in the house. There was room for expansion because of the huge basement with its high ceilings and a second wood-burning fireplace. It was just begging to be finished, and indeed it was within the first couple of years: there was a big rec room that was paneled (of course), nine-by-nine-inch white acoustical ceiling tiles, and a checkerboard of colored twelve-by-twelve floor tiles (both containing asbestos!). Thankfully, a second bathroom with a shower and vanity area were also added. The unfinished side of the basement contained a laundry room (with washer and dryer AND clothes lines), storage areas, and a large walk-in cedar closet. The finished basement literally doubled our square footage. The upstairs was relegated to the folks—the basement was ours. The age of rock and roll was upon us, and over the years, we blasted many a 45 on the phonograph down there.

When our summer vacation ended, Jerry would be off to Cretin High School. Summer vacations were long back then—from mid-May until just after Labor Day. Oh, how I loved summers. That fall, my new walk to school didn't seem so bad. Unfortunately, as you may have heard, winter has a tendency to follow fall. And in Minnesota, I mean WINTER.

Because I had to walk around a portion of Como Lake to get to school, I faced a northwest wind that whistled across it. There were no busses or car pools…it was suck it up and bundle up or freeze. Remember Ralphie's little brother in *A Christmas Story*? That's what I looked like all winter.

Dad finally broke down and bought Mom her own car—a dark-blue '46 Ford two-door coupe. It had a flathead V8 with three on the tree (a straight stick manual transmission with the shifting on the steering column for you younger folks).

Who's the New Kid?

"Class, I'd like you to meet Susie Bachmeier," said Miss Elm, our seventh grade non-nun English and penmanship teacher. "Susie's family just moved here, and she has transferred from St. Bernard's."

And there she stood in front of the class—tall, freckled faced, reddish-brown hair, and a big grin that revealed a somewhat off kilter front tooth. I gazed at her and thought to myself, *Now she's just about the cutest girl I have ever seen.*

The year was 1958—and the "Greasers" were considered by a lot of the kids to be very cool (think Fonzy from *Happy Days*). Few adults, however, shared that sentiment. They said that "Greasers" were nothing more than "Hoods," which, I guess, was short for hoodlum. But few "Greasers" were actually hoodlums, toughs, or trouble makers—at least I wasn't. We were just into that cool look. Let me paint you a picture: low-slung blue jeans rolled up at the bottom to form cuffs, black engineer boots, a wide black belt with the buckle worn on the left side, a tee-shirt with a pack of cigarettes rolled up under one sleeve, a cigarette behind one ear, long greasy hair slicked back into a duck tail, a pompadour hanging down over the forehead, and the newest and best fads of all—sideburns and a curled-up lip smirk (thank you, Elvis). Well, okay, growing sideburns at thirteen was indeed a challenge, but I had the combination lip curl-smirk/ sneer totally perfected. Oh, let's not forget that when there was even the slightest chill in the air, out came the leather jacket…and the collar was ALWAYS turned up.

I discovered that there were many people who were not long-hair fans…and that included the Notre Dame nuns at St. Andrew's. Shortly after Miss Bachmeier's introduction, I was faced with a most serious dilemma: after serving mass one Sunday morning, I was leaving church by a side door when a hand reached out and roughly grabbed my right shoulder—it was Sister William Marie and she seemed to be a tad vexed. "Okay, Mr. Golden, it's time to either get a haircut or get out of the altar boys." Well, I rather enjoyed serving mass, but on the other hand, there was this new girl that I greatly wanted to impress. Could that be done with short hair? I thought not. So, with that in mind, I had made my decision… "Sister, I am NOT going to get a haircut, so I guess I'll just have to quit the altar boys." She stood there glaring at me for a minute and then said, "Okay—you're out," and she walked away. I felt kind of bad but quickly got over it. After all, I had a new challenge to concentrate on.

St. Andrew's School, Class 1959

It sure felt like it was love at first sight. Now you may be thinking *"LOVE"* at thirteen? More like puppy love. (Paul Anka made a lot of money singing about it.) Well, okay, maybe it was just puppy love; but with heart palpitations, shortness of breath, and a tingly sensation when I looked at her, I sure thought it was love. It wasn't long after that I told some friends that I intended to marry her. Quite the decision for a seventh grader.

Now I'm sure that my steady gaze on the new kid didn't go unnoticed by our teacher, Miss Elm. She was a woman in her fifties that had never married and lived a most quiet, sedate, and secluded life with her mother. Extraordinarily dedicated and demanding, she expected her students to behave and to learn. She had little tolerance for any fooling around in her class, and disruptors were quickly dispatched to the principal's office. She insisted on getting the proper respect—and in hindsight, she deserved it. She often challenged the students to *"Dare to be different."* At thirteen, I'm not sure we really appreciated that bit of advice, but over the years, I have often reflected on that phrase. Anyway, if she did notice me ogling my true love, to her credit, she never said a word.

31

Susie and her family had moved to Como from the Rice St. and Maryland Ave. area of St. Paul. They had been members of St. Bernard's parish and all the Bachmeier kids, who were old enough, had gone to school there. They had moved into one of the large old houses on West Como Blvd. It sat high on a hill overlooking the lake. Now I should explain that Como Lake is small and may not even be large enough to be counted as one of Minnesota's ten thousand lakes. It's only sixty-eight acres and one of several lakes tucked inside of St. Paul's city limits. At just over 1.5 miles around, it was, and continues to be, quite popular with walkers, runners, and bikers. Back then the lake had both a paved walking path and a roadway encircling it. Early evenings during the week, and especially on warm weekends, you'd see couples with their kids and dog(s) in tow on the walking path. They'd wave at people sitting on their front porches and always get a return wave. The Bachmeier house had a large front porch across the front, but it was enclosed so you really couldn't see if anybody was out on it.

On Sundays, I'd see Susie's whole family at mass… Mom, Dad, and six kids. No longer an altar boy, I was free to look and dream all during the church service. But I have to admit, the sight of her super-sized daddy standing there intimidated me a bit.

Baby It's Cold Outside

Winters in Minnesota tend to be both long and frigid. The lakes generally freeze over in November and don't thaw until late April. With so many lakes, I guess it only natural that skating was, and is, quite popular. Despite the extremely cold weather, nearly all the skating rinks were outside, making appropriate attire a must. Today, most every rink is indoors.

Each winter Como Lake had three separate side-by-side skating rinks: the first was a large oval race track specifically designed for speed skating, the second was a general-purpose rink open to all skaters, the third was a regulation-size hockey rink with nets and surrounded by wooden boards. Here's the best part…all three rinks were lit at night.

As temperatures could be brutal, we were fortunate that Como Lake had a lakeside pavilion. It was a large pillared concrete structure built into the side of a small hill next to the water. The main facility housed a large wooden stage used primarily for concerts in the warm months. It had an expansive seating area that was filled with long green portable benches. In the summer, there was also a small restaurant open inside the building. Below all that was the lower lakeside level (kind of a walk-out basement). In the winter, it housed the warming house for the skaters. A wooden walkway connected the lake ice to the warming house. The walkway was divided by a center hand rail in order to make a one-way lane in each direction—to and from the lake.

The warming house was a large open room with whitewashed concrete walls and wooden benches around the perimeter. The concrete floor was covered in rubber matting to protect the blades edges, but most skaters also had skate guards. In the event that you needed sharpening, it was available for a price (providing the guy actually showed up).

Como Lake Pavilion

The simple room was designed to be a functional and comfortable place to put on and take off your skates, to warm up, and to get a bite to eat. There was a refreshment stand against the wall that served snacks including hot dogs, hot chocolate, coffee, pop, candy, and, of course, popcorn. Upon entering, you were immediately hit with the smells of popcorn, cigarette smoke, and the smoke emanating from a pot-bellied wood-burning stove that sat in the middle of the room. It was the only heat source, and it glowed red from the raging fire inside. The guy responsible for stoking that fire, adding wood, running the refreshment stand, and keeping general order in the place was a one-legged guy named Vince. He was very good-looking and probably in his mid-twenties. I had been told that he lost his leg in Korea. His long blond hair was combed "greaser" style with slicked back sides ending in the best ducktail I have ever seen. He not only had sideburns, he had muttonchops. I was more than a little jealous.

On weeknights and weekends the warming house was crowded. Mixing in with the smell of popcorn and smoke, you might also get a whiff of sweat. Smoking was permitted inside with no age restrictions despite the "eighteen or older" law. I'd estimate the average age in the place was fifteen, and most everybody was puffing away—both the guys and the gals. Back in the fifties and sixties, kids could buy cigarettes almost anywhere. I think the only provisions were that you had to be tall enough to see over the store's counter and have a quarter. Cigarettes were not sold in the warming house, consequently you'd see a lot of "bumming" going on. And as for adult supervision, Vince was it. He smoked himself and really didn't care who else was smoking. Not his job. Some evenings a copy of *Catcher in the Rye* made the rounds. All of the good parts were clearly marked.

I fancied myself a decent skater, and like nearly all the guys, I had regular hockey skates. I occasionally wandered over to the speed skating rink and became aware of the "long blades." I wanted some and pleaded with my parents to get me a pair. The answer was always the same: "Too expensive." They eventually gave in, and I got a pair as a Christmas present.

I asked around at school and found out that Susie loved to skate—both ice and roller. I knew, based on this valuable intelligence, that I'd eventually see her at the Como Lake ice rink. So, after supper on most winter evenings, I'd convince my parents that my homework was all done. That allowed me to head for the lake with my skates slung over my shoulder. Ah, that cold, crisp, invigorating fresh air, the exercise… and, oh, maybe that exciting new female attraction!

I was lacing up my skates one evening when the door opened and Susie walked in wearing a baby-blue jacket with a fur-lined hood. Her white figure skates were draped over her shoulder. Her face was rosy from the cold walk from her house to the rink, and I thought she looked gorgeous. Now that she was here, how would I get her attention? Maybe a little smile and a nod…or possibly my best Elvis sneer.

I casually walked by, smiled, nodded, and headed for the ice. I skated in circles, keeping a close eye on the door. Time seemed to stand still as I waited for her to emerge. I mean how long does it take to lace up some skates? Finally, the door opened and she started down the wooden ramp. She looked like an angel in that blue jacket with the fur-trimmed hood now up and framing her face. Oh, man, was I smitten!

I skated by her and simply said, "Hi." She smiled and returned the greeting. I cruised around the rink a bit, trying to look as cool as possible, hoping she'd be watching. She wasn't. To my chagrin she was totally ignoring me and chatting with some girlfriends.

My Best Buddy

Steve McDonough was my best friend. He was a very nice guy, a non-skater, and a bit of a loner. He was tall, quite slender, had short brown hair, and wore dark-rimmed Buddy Holly glasses. He had a pretty high IQ and looked the part. Steve had a large scar under his Adam's apple, the result of once having a tracheotomy tube due to childhood polio and severe breathing problems. He hid the scar by buttoning his shirt right up to the very top—including the top button. That was thought to be very un-cool. What he may have lacked in an outer coolness, he more than made up for with his sense of humor. It could be a little sophomoric, offbeat, and sarcastic; but I thought his witty observations were very funny. His father was a Minneapolis high school history teacher and a tough disciplinarian.

Unfortunately, his mother was pretty stern as well. I wondered if there was much laughter in that home.

Nearly every Saturday morning, they left him home to babysit his younger brother while they warmed the stools of a local pub… all day and into the evening. He was just quiet, studious Steve to most, but when we were together, the laughter never stopped. As I mentioned, he had breathing problems and hanging out with me probably didn't help matters much. I introduced him to smoking. Okay, in retrospect, that was a horrible thing to do; but give me a break, I was only thirteen.

Steve was not particularly interested in girls. No, no, he was not gay. Maybe he just didn't have the same raging hormones that I had. He was not very fond of Susie or my keen interest in her. I think he viewed her as a threat to our friendship. But he needn't have worried—she didn't want anything to do with me.

Funny Stuff

I earned some money by cutting lawns and shoveling snow in the neighborhood. To that money I added my allowance, birthday cash, and change pilfered from my mother's purse. You see, I had a goal to purchase the reel-to-reel tape recorder that I had seen in Karl's TV. Karl's was primarily a neighborhood TV repair shop, but they also sold radios, portable TV's (no big console units), and recording equipment. I wanted that recorder so that Steve and I could tape some of our whacky skits that we thought were hilarious. I finally got it.

Our recording sessions were always in my basement. We never had a script…we simply agreed on a premise, and then I punched the Record button. It was total improv, and neither of us had any idea what the other would say. He might be the news anchor and I the weatherman, or I might be the rock star being interviewed by the radio DJ, or I could be the boss interviewing an applicant. It didn't matter—we would continue until one of us made the other one laugh uncontrollably. That's when I'd have to hit the STOP button. I don't know if they were as funny as we thought, but the sessions were a much-needed diversion from my Susie obsession.

Oh, Brother

Jerry was the first in the family to mimic the Elvis hair style. Dad didn't have enough hair left to copy it even if he wanted to (which he didn't), and Mom had her own thing going. No sideburns for her. That left only me. I got my desire to look cool from Jerry as well as James Dean, Tony Curtis, Elvis, the Everly Brothers, and a whole host of others. *Take a look at the family photo taken around 1960 at our paternal grandparents' fiftieth wedding anniversary.* On the left, behind a cousin, is Jerry, who is actually looking pretty dapper. NOT ME. I'm on the far right giving the camera my best James Dean squint. A pack of Camels is rolled up in my left shirt sleeve, the shirt is unbuttoned, the collar is up, and I have a smoke in my right hand. Infinite coolness. Yeah, Jerry, his buddies, and the rock idols of the day certainly had quite an influence on me. Jerry's friends called him Rocky—and me Little Rock. To this day I have no idea where the Rocky nickname came from. It seemed to disappear as quickly as it had appeared. Oh, do I have some stories to tell you about Jerry.

Forgive me if I skip around a couple of years. I vividly recall the incidents—but the actual year, not so much.

Grandma and Grampa Golden, 50ᵗʰ Wedding Anniversary

Clean Up in Aisle Two

As previously mentioned, Como Park has a big fountain near the lake and pavilion. At that time it was located in the center of a round-a-bout (while the fountain still remains, the traffic circle has been eliminated). A large round fountain pond took up the majority of the traffic circle and at its center a huge bronze mermaid statue. She is holding a cornucopia from which water shoots straight up into the air. Additional water jets are located around the perimeter of the pond. They shoot streams of water into the air that arc back down around the statue. Underwater spot lights change color and illuminate the entire fountain at night.

One evening, Jerry and a buddy thought it would be funny to pour wash machine soap into the fountain. They bought several boxes of powdered soap, and when no cars were coming, they dumped them in. Well, between the water jets and the various pumps, the pond quickly filled with suds. While he and his friend hid on the hill by the Gates Ajar observing, a Como Park squad car happened by and stopped. They notified the fire department. Do you see what's coming? Yup, the fireman, hoping to rinse away the suds, hit the fountain with fire hoses. Unfortunately, that action quickly multiplied the suds by many fold. They now spilled out into the road surrounding the fountain. Cars coming around the lake came to a complete stop at seeing the flashing red lights of the squad car and fire engine—and, of course, the bubble wall. What an awesome sight that must have been.

Caught in the Act

Our parents were outgoing, fun, and sociable people. As we got older, they would trust us to be home alone as they went off to meet with friends for various outings and activities. One summer morning, when I was eleven and Jerry fourteen, they informed us that they were going to meet friends at Metropolitan Stadium in Bloomington to see a Twins game *(Metropolitan stadium is where both the Twins and the Vikings played and is now the current site of the Mall of America).*

So, as we were watching them disappear up the street, Jerry suddenly said, "See ya." He hopped into Mom's '46 Ford Coupe and off he went (no license, no insurance, and not a care in the world). Okay by me, I was building a new model car *(more on this hobby later)*, so I retreated to the basement to work on that. I put on a stack of 45s and had the stereo blasting when I heard my father yell from the top of the stairs, "Tom, get up here." YIKES! Turns out, Dad had forgotten the baseball tickets on his dresser and had to come back for them.

"Where's Jerry?"

"I don't know."

"Where's the car?"

"I don't know."

I think I actually saw smoke come out of his ears. Off he went looking for my wayward brother. It didn't take long to find him—he was only about six blocks away. The '46 Ford was parked on a friend's lawn along with about six other cars. Oh, I would have gladly given up my allowance to have seen the look on his face when Dad pulled up. After that incident, they always took the keys for the '46 with them when they left. What they didn't know was that Jerry had already had a spare set of keys made.

Older but wiser? That remains in question to this very day. Read on.

Not Exactly a Harley

I quickly learned that when Jerry said, "Watch this," something bad was about to happen. Think I'm kidding? One day I was up at my friend Frank's house. He was working on his car that was parked in his driveway. From inside the garage a radio, tuned to KDWB, channel 63, blasted the latest in rock and roll TOP 40 hits. I just watched, and we made conversation as Frank sanded the body of his old Chevy preparing it for a re-paint.

Jerry pulled up on an old motorcycle and revved the engine. It was LOUD. He had recently purchased it from somebody in the neighborhood and was just out cruising around. He said, "Hop on." Being the idiot that I am, I did. We took off like a rocket as he hunched forward over the handlebars with me holding onto his mid-section for dear life. Then came that dreaded phrase, *"Watch this."* He opened it up all the way, and we were flying down the street far faster than I was comfortable with. The next thing I heard was, "Drag your feet."

"What?"

"DRAG YOUR FEET."

Now as I mentioned, this was an old motorcycle and the entire braking system was totally dependent on...a single cotter pin. You guessed it—the cotter pin had snapped, and we were blazing down the road with zero ability to stop. A block ahead was Grotto Street... and a STOP sign. Being a good Catholic I began, "Hail Mary, full of grace..." Well, we sailed right through that stop sign without injury or death. Thankfully, there had been no cross traffic. But we weren't out of the woods yet because just ahead was Dale Street, a red light, and LOTS of cross traffic. He was now downshifting gears to reduce the speed while continuing to yell, "Drag your feet." Forget the Hail Mary's—it was now Act of Contrition time. Somehow, someway, with smoking soles on our shoes, we managed to finally come to a complete stop just before entering the intersection. I immediately hopped off and began walking. "Hey," he hollered, "don't you want a ride back to Frank's house?" I didn't even look back.

Henry Ford Would Be So Proud

A little later on he had a customized candy apple-red 1951 Ford coupe. It had the Ford flathead V8 engine with a manual transmission that originally shifted from the steering column, but that was certainly not good enough. The shifter MUST be floor mounted on the transmission hump. So it had been converted. Now when I say the car was customized, I mean it had all the body chrome removed: it was nosed, decked, had a louvered hood, and chrome lake pipes were mounted on the sides just under the rocker panels. The car was lowered all around to the point of nearly dragging on the ground *(getting in and out of gas stations was a real challenge)*. The door handles had also been removed and replaced with electrical solenoid buttons: on the outside they were mounted near the windshield wipers; on the inside they were on the dashboard. These electrical buttons played a key role in two stories I'm about to share. Both should have resulted in death.

Story 1: Jerry's girlfriend, Marion, also lived in the Como Park area just a mile or so from our house. One late afternoon, on a cool fall day, he was headed over to her place. As usual, he was slumped in the corner, leaning heavily against the driver's door. All cool guys drove that way—you never wanted to be seen sitting up straight in your car. As he maneuvered through the residential neighborhood, he downshifted into second as he made a right turn—his full body weight against the driver's door. That pressure, coupled with the centrifugal force resulting from turning with too much speed, caused the door latch to give way and the driver's side door flew open. His fancy customized car literally spit him out onto the pavement. There he was, lying in the street, watching as his car went merrily along all by itself.

Thankfully, he had not been run over and his greaser leather jacket saved him from getting some nasty road rash. Nothing hurt other than his pride. But now the race was on...he had to catch up to his run-away car, hop in, and stop it before it hit a parked car or a tree or a HOUSE!

Well, that's where the wonderment of the manual transmission comes in. The car had been in second gear as he rounded the corner so with no pressure on the gas pedal and nobody to press down on the clutch pedal, the car began to chug violently as it slowed down. In my opinion, this should be publicized as an important safety feature when comparing the manual transmission to the automatic transmission: _"Safety Tip: In the event that you fall out of your Camaro..."_ Thankfully, he was able to outrun the jerking car and jump back in before any damage was caused. Where were the smart phones with video capabilities when you really needed them? That car chase would have been an Internet sensation.

Story 2: Back then, police patrol cars each had two partner officers. They were assigned to the same neighborhood beat day in and day out. Because of this routine, they knew (or knew of) every teenager who lived in the vicinity. They also knew what kind of a car each drove. They were well aware of Jerry…and his hot rod Ford.

The crime rate in Como Park neighborhoods was nearly non-existent so that afforded them the time to stop teenage drivers for assorted driving infractions: speeding, squealing tires, loud exhaust (the actual purpose of lake pipes), burnt-out lights, etc. And let's face it, on occasion, they pulled some kids over just for the sheer fun of it.

One sunny but chilly morning (I say chilly because all of the car windows had been rolled up), I was riding shotgun in the '51 Ford when Jerry said, *"Watch this."* Oh crap! The Ford came equipped with a flathead V8 and a single two-barrel carburetor. Like Tim the tool man Taylor used to growl, "More power." So Jerry had installed tri-carbs with progressive linkage (meaning the original single two-barrel carburetor was replaced with THREE two-barrel carburetors). The engine would run on the center two-barrel carb until the gas pedal was punched—then the other two would kick in with a roar and suck down gas like you owned an oil well. The *"watch this"* warning was followed by him stomping on the accelerator, thus causing all three carbs to roar into action. Unfortunately, a gas line popped and spewed gas all over the engine. That quickly caught fire and smoke billowed out the front grill, the louvres in the hood, and then began pouring inside the car from beneath the dash. Remember those electronic solenoid door openers? One minor problem, they don't work once the electrical system melts.

With no interior door handles to open the doors, we frantically cranked down the windows as the car began filling with smoke. At that very moment, the squad car containing the two Como Park "protect and serve" police officers pulled up and stopped alongside. They looked, and then they laughed. Seeing that we had open windows from which to escape, they drove off. We did indeed bail out through the windows. Jerry grabbed a fire extinguisher from the trunk, popped the hood, and doused the engine flames before the entire car was engulfed. We hand pushed it the four blocks back to the front of our house.

Model Cars

I was not exactly anti-social, but I did enjoy my alone time listening to records and building model cars in the basement of our house. I had laid claim to a corner of the room that I furnished with an old chest of drawers that I filled with all my model car kits, model car parts, numerous bottles and cans of paint, tubes of Testor's glue and plastic wood, X-ACTO knives, sandpaper, etc. Next to the chest of drawers I had a square card table that was spattered with various paint colors, dried glue, plastic wood, and had numerous cuts made by the X-ACTO knife blade. An overhead basement window and a desk lamp lit the area. Dad had also salvaged an old desk chair from Brown & Bigelow for me. It was my very own little corner of the world, and I loved it.

I would use my allowance money, as well as the money earned doing chores around the neighborhood, to buy the model car kits. I never wanted my model cars, however, to look anything like the photo on the box. My cars all had to be uniquely customized, with some radically re-designed. To make those modifications I needed the use of a product called plastic wood (a wood filler in a tube). I used it to mold and shape my designs; fill holes on the models; form new fenders; grill openings, headlights and taillights, roof lines, etc. Just squeeze it out of the tube (it came out thick, like peanut butter), then form it as desired. It dried hard, and the process could take many thin layers with some sanding in between. When I was finally satisfied, I would do a final sanding with a fine-grit sandpaper, then apply a coat of primer. It was now ready for the final coat(s) of paint. Tedious and exacting work to be sure, but when I was finished, the cars were (allow me to brag) magnificent. I wasn't so much a model car builder as a car designer. I had several examples of my handiwork on display in the front windows of two different hobby shops—one in downtown St. Paul and the other in the Como Park area. My models also won blue ribbons at the Minnesota State Fair.

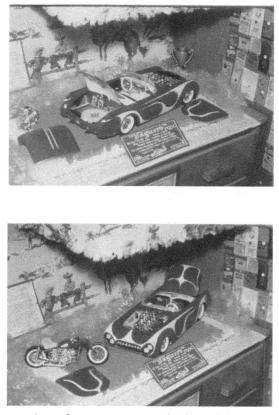

One of my many custom-built model cars

In order to make each car unique, I often swapped out parts from one car kit to use on a car from a different kit. In fact, it got to the point that I'd look at the model car box photo and think I really only want that grill, or that bumper, or that dashboard. I had boxes of parts: grills, bumpers, wheels and tires, interiors, etc. It was my very own miniature auto salvage yard. That "parts only" mentality is how I turned an innocent hobby into big trouble. I didn't want to spend my hard-earned money to purchase an entire car kit when all I really wanted was a few of the parts in the box. So… I bet you are way ahead of me, aren't you?

One Saturday, Dad asked if I wanted to go with him to Hub Center, a strip shopping center containing about a dozen stores in Roseville (the first tier suburb north of St. Paul). Remember, these were the pre-mall days, and even though downtown St. Paul and Minneapolis were still very vibrant, steady movement to the suburbs was leading to the development of many "convenience strip centers."

A brief retail history lesson: The country's very first enclosed mall was built in 1956 in the upscale Minneapolis suburb of Edina. It's called Southdale. That first "dale" eventually led to Rosedale, Brookdale, Ridgedale, and numerous other Twin City malls. The Hub strip center, located in Roseville, became part of the first mall developed on the St. Paul side of the Twin Cities. It was called Har Mar Mall, and it was built on the former site of Harkin's golf driving range. The somewhat odd mall name was derived from the combination of the owners/developers first names... **HAR**old and **MAR**ie Slawik. Before I conclude this retail history lesson, let me just add that west of Har Mar Mall, across Snelling Avenue, was the nation's first *Best Buy Company* (originally called the *Sound of Music*). Then just north of Har Mar Mall, across County Road B, was the nation's first *Target* store. Yes, the Twin Cities was indeed a beehive of retail innovation.

Okay, back to Hub Center: I went with dad that Saturday morning with about $3 in my pocket (big money in those days). He went off to the bank and the dry cleaners while I wandered into the hardware store. Against the back wall were all kinds of model kits and various supplies needed to assemble and finish them. I looked at one kit, which I clearly had enough money to buy, and admired the grill and wheels as shown on the box cover. Those were the only parts that I wanted, so I opened the box and fished around for them. Nobody seemed to be watching me, so I grabbed the parts and stuffed them into my coat pocket. As I nonchalantly walked toward the front door, I heard a loud voice from behind me yell, "Hey, you—**STOP**." I looked around, and a man was quickly moving toward me. I panicked. I pushed the door open and ran outside and directly into my father. I mean, I literally ran right into him and almost knocked him down. He looked at me and then at the screaming man who was chasing me out of the store. Yeah, funny now—terrifying then.

After a conversation between the store manager and my father, we all went back inside where I paid for the entire car kit. I got a lecture from the store manager and was then released into the custody of my father.

As I mentioned earlier, Dad was a pretty big guy—especially to a child. He had been quite athletic in his day and had been a championship softball pitcher. That meant a very strong right arm and right hand. Even as an "old man" in his forties, he was still in relatively decent shape. When he got mad, he tended to turn bright red and shout quite loudly. Sometimes he'd get so angry that he'd actually shake. Pretty scary stuff for a kid. He rarely struck me or Jerry—it was just the threat of getting smacked.

On this particular occasion, he stayed surprisingly calm. That didn't fit the pattern that I was used to. I had fully expected he would yell at me all the way home. But instead, he simply asked why I had done it. I tried to explain, but let's face it, there simply was no excuse. I said I was sorry, and he responded that he was both embarrassed by my actions and disappointed in me. Then he just said, "Don't ever do anything like that again." I promised that I wouldn't, and that was the end of it. I have never stolen anything since…but I was an accessory to a theft.

45 RPM

I was with a buddy named Jim, and we had been hanging out all day at the zoo and wandering around the park. For some reason, we decided to walk the two miles or so from Como Park out to a Roseville shopping area (no, not Hub Center, but a much closer and similar string of stores). In the fifties and sixties, nearly every kind of retailer sold 45 rpm records for 88 cents. Most stores only carried the current Top 40 hits so the record racks didn't take up too much floor space. So Jim and I walked into a grocery store and went over to the record rack. As we flipped through the records, I saw Jim slip one under his jacket. It was "Bye, Bye Love" by the Everly Brothers. He looked at me and said, "Let's go." We both headed for the automatic doors. Just as the out-door began to open, we became aware of a man wearing a white shirt, a black bow tie, and a green apron moving quickly in our direction. As the door swung open, we bolted through it and began to run—that's when Jim pulled the record out from under his coat and handed it to me. For reasons that are still totally beyond my comprehension, I actually took it. Jim was faster than me as was the store manager. I was grabbed from behind (shades of Sister William Marie and the hardware store owner) and escorted back inside still clutching the stolen 45.

The guy was pretty angry and treated me as if I had committed the crime of the century. He knew that I wasn't the actual thief, but I was an accomplice and the only one in custody! I told him that I had no idea that my friend intended to steal the record (which was the truth), but I also refused to identify Jim, which annoyed him even more. After grilling me in his office for a while he decided to call the Roseville police. Two cops arrived, and they took turns questioning me about the crime. They tried to scare me into identifying Jim, but I continued to refuse. After some paperwork was filled out, the cops and the grocery store manager stepped out into the hallway and had a quiet conversation. I was then escorted out of the store and put into the back of the squad car. I thought I was going to the Roseville police station, but to my surprise, they told me that they had convinced the store manager not to press charges and they were going to drive me home. Small world, lucky for me, one of the cops had gone to Cretin with Dad. One of those "it's not *what* you know, it's *who* you know" deals.

My poor mother…she answered the doorbell only to see me standing in between two Roseville police officers with very serious expressions on their faces. After they explained what had happened, she assured them that I was a good boy and that it would never happen again. I hung my head in shame as they left, and she just looked at me and said, "Wait 'til your father gets home." Oh no, and after I had promised him that I would never steal anything again. At least this time there were extenuating circumstances. To the best of my knowledge, she never told him.

Needless to say, Jim and I ceased to be friends.

Tough Guys

I was involved in very few fist fights while attending St. Andrew's. Maybe because I had that "hood" look, nobody wanted to test me. I wasn't really all that tough, but I always exuded confidence and acted as if I was. I never backed down, and that made others think twice before ever confronting me. Well, that is, except for Jerome. He was the tallest kid in our class and, at one time, one of my best friends. For some long-forgotten reason, we got into it. I should have known better than to think I could beat him in a fight as he was much taller, heavier, and had a reach far greater than mine. But as I said, I never backed down. So at recess, out on the playground, we mixed it up. It was over in seconds. I was lying on the asphalt and he stood towering triumphantly over me while nearly the entire class gathered around. Talk about humiliating. A nun came running over to break it up, but it was already over. When I finally got back on my feet, she insisted that Jerome and I shake hands. We begrudgingly did, but we were no longer friends. We both ended up going to Cretin, but we simply avoided each other for four years.

Now that I had gotten my clock cleaned in front of a rather large audience, a well-known public school hot shot named Russ heard about my playground fiasco. I had no particular gripe with Russ, and I didn't think that he had one with me. We were never friends, but we lived just a few blocks apart, and we had always been civil to each other. You know, just a smile and a nod, or a "hey, how are you" kind of thing. Both he and his older brother had reputations as being neighborhood tough guys, but they had left me alone—until now.

It might have been one of those "blood in the water" deals, or maybe he just wanted to impress the other neighborhood kids. I don't have any idea why Russ thought it was a good idea to pick a fight with me, but pick a fight he did. And it was in front of witnesses.

The Hang-Out

Nick's Grocery Store was a neighborhood convenience shop run by a short, slightly built Italian immigrant named Nick. He was in his fifties, and as a result of years of holding and chain-smoking unfiltered cigarettes, his olive-colored complexion was badly wrinkled and his right index and middle fingers were darkly stained an orange color. Funny, I can't remember if he smoked Camels or Lucky Strike—but you can bet is was one of the two. All the neighborhood kids liked to gather both inside and outside of the store. Nick hated that because he was convinced that it was scaring off customers. He was probably right, but as he sold us cigarettes, he kind of invited the problem.

There were large plate-glass windows on the front of the store plastered with "Specials" signs. Despite those, you could still clearly see inside from the street and sidewalk. Inside the store, pushed up against those big windows, were a couple of large silver metal pop coolers. Those coolers were not the upright dispensing machines of today, but rather large chest-type units with big heavy sliding metal doors on the top. They were perfect for sitting on.

When adult customers parked at the curb, they often saw a group of teenagers standing around outside the store smoking and a bunch of teenagers inside the store doing the same. We'd love to sit on those silver pop coolers drinking Coke or Pepsi and eating either Twinkies or one of two competing brands of small round baked fruit pies. Those apple and cherry pies were great, and we argued as to which brand was better... Paramount or Rainbow. So there we sat, eating, drinking, puffing away, talking and laughing until the group got so large that Nick could no longer stand it. He would storm out from behind the counter that held the cash register and rush towards us, jabbing his right index finger into the air while yelling with his thick Italian accent, *"Ah-one, ah-two, ah-three—getta yo ass outta here."* We'd all just sit for a minute and stare at him to be sure he was serious. When his color began to turn purple we knew it was time to leave. We'd walk outside and wait around the front for a while. Then one by one, we'd casually wander back in. Oh, we all knew that it would just be a matter of time before Nick blew again, but it was a game for us. Not so sure it was for Nick.

One evening, after being thrown out of the store, the group gathered outside and it included Russ and his older brother. I ignored them and was chatting away with some buddies. Russ came over and said, "I heard that you were pretty tough." I said, "Yup." He continued, "I also heard that you got the crap kicked out of you at school, so maybe you aren't so tough after all." I said, "Tough enough." Then came those call to action words… "Prove it." Much to my own surprise I decked him with a single right hook. The blow connected full force dead center between his mouth and nose, and that pretty much took all the fight out of him. He stayed on the ground for quite a while, and I suspect that he may have been seeing stars. A few of us then went back inside Nick's as Russ got up and left with a bloody nose, bloody mouth, bruised ego…and his brother. I thought to myself, *I know exactly how you feel.*

Word spread about that encounter, and I had new respect in the neighborhood despite my recent humiliation on the school playground. I was never challenged again. That was my very last fight.

As angry as Nick used to get, yelling, swearing, and shaking his finger at us, he also watched out for us. Maybe it was because he felt that while our presence may discourage some customers, it did the same for armed robbers. I'd prefer to think it was because he secretly liked us.

One evening, right at the dinner table, Jerry and Dad got into a very heated argument. Both were shouting at each other as I and my mother just watched. It got physical. Dad slammed Jerry up against the refrigerator; but Jerry, now nearly his same size, pushed back. And I mean HARD. Then he quickly stormed out of the house. After Dad had cooled down, he went out looking for Jerry. Not to apologize mind you, he never ever admitted to being wrong, but simply to bring him home. His first logical stop was Nick's. He walked into the store, looked at all the teens who were gathered there, and asked, "Hey, Nick, have you seen Jerry?" Nick replied, "Nope." Jerry heard everything as he hid in the dark at the bottom of the basement stairs.

Island of Love

Well, to be honest, it was actually a peninsula rather than an island.

Winter evenings in Minnesota are not just cold, but they can be strikingly beautiful as well. If the skies are clear, you can see millions of twinkling stars with a brilliance that is beyond belief (and, on rare occasion, you may even see the aura borealis—also known as northern lights). I'm talking star-gazing frostbite here, unless, of course, you had your love to keep you warm (plus a boatload of layered clothing). On some occasions, I was fortunate enough to have both.

I continued to pursue Susie at school, at the skating rink, and by going over to her house and brazenly knocking on her back door. Her mother seemed to like me, but her father wasn't at all pleased by my constant visits. But I persisted, and Susie eventually got friendlier. I assumed it was due to the fact that I was handsome, dashing, and charming—but more likely it was just to irritate her dad.

As I mentioned, Como Lake is relatively small compared to most lakes in the state. I read somewhere that the lake used to be somewhat larger and surrounded by farm crops and cattle. As the farms eventually turned into park land, a city parks department engineer must have said, "Hey, let's build a Florida shaped peninsula out into the water." Brilliant idea! The peninsula was built, and everybody loved it. It was especially popular with teenagers after dark.

To get to the skating rinks from my house, I had to walk several blocks, then across the main road encircling the lake, then over the peninsula, and finally out onto the lake. Sometimes the walk would be on bare slippery ice; other times I had to trudge through deep snow. Either way, I truly loved that walk. Looking up at the stars, then across the lake at the brightly lit skating rinks, just lifted my spirits. There was always a feeling of excitement, anticipation, and the promise of romance. My intention was always to kiss Susie, but I didn't want to try doing so in front of a whole bunch of skaters. What if she slapped me? That could trigger laughter, hoots and hollers, and ongoing teasing at school. Kissing her in a more secluded location seemed like a much better idea.

I'd not only heard about, but also witnessed some couples going over to the peninsula to make out. It was in the dark and out of eyesight from the lighted skating rinks. On the other hand, everybody could see you heading over that way—or coming back. It could be difficult reaching "the point" if the snow was deep and you had your skates on. Nevertheless, people managed to do it. Couples would sneak over there, sit on the big boulders or the concrete curbing surrounding the peninsula's outer edge, and…well, they'd kiss. What a wonderful and stimulating idea—but would Susie actually go over there with me?

To keep warm, I'd wear long underwear, two pairs of socks, a sweater, a scarf, earmuffs, gloves or mittens, the leather jacket, and, on rare occasions, a stocking cap. The cap was a last resort because it messed up my hair. When you removed your cap inside the warming house, sometimes the static electricity made your hair stand straight up. Definitely not a good look. Despite all the cold weather clothing, your face was almost always exposed to the elements. Some kids wore the stocking caps that could be pulled down over the face. I never liked them. They had eye holes and a nose/mouth hole, and they really looked awful (but they were pretty popular with the criminal element).

If it was bitterly cold (below zero), I would wrap a scarf around my face but that, as you can well imagine, made it difficult to talk, not to mention breathe. So with a scarf around your nose, mouth and chin, the only thing left uncovered and exposed were your eyes. If you have never experienced being outside in below zero temperatures, you may think that I am making this up—but I'm not. Air that cold makes your eyes water, and that quickly turns to ice on your eyelashes. Yes, it can quite literally freeze your eyes shut. To prevent that from happening, you'd have to remove your glove or mitten, squeeze your eyelash between your bare thumb and index finger, and pull the ice off. I can see Southerners shaking their heads and thinking, *Is he serious?* You bet I am—just ask a Northerner (or a Yankee).

Hmmm—a Northerner or Yankee—aren't they the same thing? As it turns out, NO. As a Southern transplant, I've been told by natives that Yankees are from the East Coast. Northerners, on the other hand, are from places like the Midwest. Many years ago a friend named Don, who was born and raised in Baton Rouge, informed me that I hailed from the "uppa US." He's the same guy who once called me with one of the funniest lines that I have ever heard. Baton Rouge was experiencing some horrible Mississippi river flooding. Meanwhile, upstream in Minnesota, there were no such problems. My office phone rang one day, and this is what I heard when I answered, "Golden, Don here. Stop flushing." Then he hung up.

But I digress. Back to facial warmth in the tundra.

One evening out on the skating rink, I got up the courage to ask Susie if she'd like to skate with me out to "the point." I couldn't believe it—she smiled and agreed. As we moved closer and closer to that little strip of land, my heart began pounding. It was also about that same time that I realized that my nose was running. Well, c'mon, it was cold. So what was going through my head was the thought of kissing her with a runny cold nose. Exactly how magical and romantic would she find that experience?

I took off my right glove and pulled a handkerchief from my leather jacket pocket. I got in the habit of carrying one because I suffered from hay fever from late August until the first freeze. It was just nice to have something handy to blow my nose into. A lot of guys carried them back then. Just watch an old movie—when some poor woman begins crying, there is always some guy there to offer her a nice, clean, crisply folded and ironed white hanky. Well, mine was a little off-white, wrinkled, un-folded, and simply stuffed in a wad into my coat pocket. But I needed to use it, not offer it to a damsel in distress. So I wiped my nose, and while the glove was off, I peeled the ice off my eyelashes. Gotta love Minnesota.

We sat on the concrete outer edge curbing of the peninsula, and I put my arm around her. We just looked at each other for a moment and right then and there I moved in for my first Susie kiss. She kind of giggled, but we kissed some more. I liked it—but at that point the jury was still out on whether or not she did.

We were both freezing, so we skated back toward the rink and the heat in the warming house. As we emerged from the darkness into the light, we got some stares from the skaters who knew us. Let's face it, you only went out to the point for one reason—to make-out. So were Tom and Susie now a couple? I went into the warming house while she stayed outside and talked to her girlfriends. I can only imagine the conversation: "What happened out there—and don't leave out any details." Guys are different. My buddies didn't pry but did expect that at some point I'd fill them in. After all, I hadn't exactly hidden the fact that I had been aggressively pursuing Susie since she was first introduced in class. I guess they felt that they deserved to know how the romance was progressing.

Chapter 2

Chapter 2

Minnesota State Fair

The state fair ran for ten days each year *(now twelve days)* from the end of August into early September. It always ends on Labor Day. Its slogan is "The Great Minnesota Get-Together," and its symbol is a Gopher *(Minnesota is the gopher state)* named Fairchild. He wears a green-and-white striped hat and matching sport coat *(sometimes a black vest too)*.

The fairgrounds consist of 320 acres located in the community of Falcon Heights, a suburb on the west side of St. Paul *(and some of you thought that Minneapolis was St. Paul's western suburb)*. Okay, to be fair *(get it?)*, the fairgrounds are physically located on the St. Paul side of the Mississippi River, but nearly dead center between downtown St. Paul and downtown Minneapolis. It has always ranked as one of the largest state fairs in the country, but over the years, it has grown substantially. It now ranks number 1 in average daily attendance *(over 150,000)* and number 2 in total annual attendance *(two million)*, behind only Texas.

State-fair time filled me with mixed emotions: on one hand, the fair was always fun and exciting, but on the other hand, fall was also the time of year when my hay fever kicked in. Plus, after Labor Day, it was back to school. The hay fever was dreadful. I'd constantly sneeze, rub my itching bloodshot eyes, and blow my nose. I was miserable until the first frost. Thankfully, I eventually outgrew my allergies.

There was, and still is, an entrance fee to the fairgrounds. Back then, before it got so insanely crowded, you could actually drive in and pay for your car and each car occupant. You'd either have to find a parking place on the outer fringe or be lucky enough to find one of the few spaces on the streets designated for parking. That could be a real hassle, especially when it got more crowded in the afternoon and evening. Most folks simply chose to park somewhere on one of the residential neighborhood streets and walk to the gates to buy their entry tickets. If you lived anywhere in the area, you probably dreaded fair time. Some folks, however, made lemonade out of the lemons. They allowed parking in the yards and on their driveways for a fee. It could be a pretty nice source of extra income. All cash—no credit cards, and probably no IRS tax declarations either.

As a kid money was always limited, and we didn't want to waste it by paying an entry fee. We wanted to keep our money to buy food on a stick and for the rides on the giant Midway. But getting in free could be a challenge. There were walls and fences encircling the entire fairgrounds. Mounted police officers monitored the exterior perimeter to discourage kids like us from getting in without paying.

Part of the excitement was when scouting for a way in, you'd spot a policeman on horseback heading in your direction. It was an adrenalin rush. We'd scatter, then duck down and hide behind something until he had ridden past. Once the coast was clear, we'd continue our search.

There was a type of grapevine amongst kids, and you always heard about where somebody had recently discovered or created a way in. There were various entry methods: (1) It could be a ditch dug under the fence. That was the "get your clothes dirty" way in. Holes under the fence were easily spotted from horseback and quickly repaired); (2) an opening in the cyclone fence created by somebody with wire snips (not always quickly discovered providing that the entrants bothered to bend the fence back in place); (3) a place to climb up and over the fence or wall; and then there was (4) "you better have some guts and running skills" for this method called *crashing the gate*. You walked up to the entrance by the ticket takers or alongside a car that was entering and then ran like hell into the crowds inside. You were rarely chased, but it did happen once in a while.

Once inside there were food booths galore: Pronto Pups (corn dogs), Rainbow ice cream cones, Tom Thumb mini-donuts, buttered corn on the cob, burgers and fries, pizza, footlong hot dogs, chocolate chip cookies, and on and on. There were hundreds of streetside food booths throughout the fairgrounds. Most were owned and operated by local residents who manned their booths annually to supplement their income. After the fair was over, they boarded up their little business venture, and it would sit idle until the next year. There was one stand over by the Hippodrome (where there were horse and cattle shows). It was sponsored by the Minnesota Dairy Association and sold "all you can drink" milk for ten cents. *(It may cost a little more today!)*

Every politician in the state made at least one appearance at the fair. There were multiple political booths strategically located within a block or two of the main entrance. Both the DFL and the GOP had large ones as did the labor unions. From the governor to the dogcatcher—each one wanted to shake your hand and give you some kind of brochure. I often thought that these booths caused more fairgoers to get nauseous than the Midway rides.

There were plenty of free exhibits ranging from horticulture to art, butter sculptures to farm machinery, and quilts to model cars (!). There were performance stages featuring everything from rock to polka. Machinery hill (really not much of a hill—more like a slight incline) had tractors, combines, various kinds of farm implements, silos and storage facilities, plus some of the very latest automobiles. *(Remember when all the new cars were introduced in September?)* Not all car brands, mind you, but enough to draw attention. New American cars and trucks were proudly displayed but no imports that I can recall.

A huge grandstand sits in the middle of the fairgrounds. I don't know what the seating capacity was back in the fifties and sixties, but I recently read that it now seats 17,000. In front of all those seats *is*, or possibly *was*, an oval race track. If you were anywhere on the fairgrounds during the afternoon, you could hear the roar of car engines as either stock cars or midget racers zoomed around and around. On the infield there's a huge stage on which name entertainers performed, and continue to perform, each evening of the fair. Let me be clear, I'm not suggesting that it's the exact same entertainers performing today as back in the fifties and sixties, although there may be a few old timers who still limp out on stage. There's nothing like watching an eighty-plus-year old singer clinging to a walker belting out "Shake, Rattle and Roll." I can say that because I'm a geezer myself!

There was a beer garden on one corner (I was too young) and a kiddie ride park on the other (I was too old) at the entrance to the MIDWAY. The ground on the Midway was covered with small wood chips and sawdust to hold down dust and to soak up spills. The blaring music was deafening; and upon entering you were immediately accosted by carnival barkers who wanted you to toss rings onto bottles, break balloons, knock over cupie dolls or stacked metal milk bottles, toss pennies onto plates, or shoot moving metal ducks. If successful, you got a worthless trinket of some sort. Like Steve Martin said in the movie *The Jerk*, *"Oh, it's one of those profit deals."*

Like most midways and carnivals, there were also the side shows/ freak shows featuring things like the five hundred-pound hairy half ape-half woman, a two-headed cow, and a slithering reptile man. All guaranteed to be REAL. Then there was the guy who could swallow flaming swords, the mirrored fun house, and so many more "take-your-breath-away attractions," all wanting your hard-earned money in exchange for a thrill.

Oh, you say you came for the rides? Well, on this mammoth midway, there were quite literally dozens of them. At night, all of them were ablaze in multicolored neon. Most whirled you around so violently that you'd exit dizzy and ready to toss your cookies. I always preferred the considerably more tame double Ferris wheel. When you were at the very top, you could see the entire fairgrounds. At night, that was quite the spectacle.

Driver's Ed

When the state fair ended, most of the fairgrounds stood empty. Oh, there might be a few small events now and then, but it was pretty much a ghost town.

Dad began taking Jerry out there when he was twelve to give him driving lessons. When I turned twelve, he did the same for me. Obviously, at that age, neither of us had a learner's permit. To Dad, that was just a mere technicality. He had been driving since he was thirteen (when no license was required), and he felt that we were ready to learn despite what the state of Minnesota might legislate. Lessons were usually on a Saturday morning or a Sunday afternoon. There were few, if any, other cars around; so we had the place to ourselves. He wanted us to be experienced drivers by the time we were old enough to get an actual license.

He taught us how to use the clutch and shift gears, make proper (not wide) turns, drive at the posted speed limit, ALWAYS use turn signals *(boy, couldn't most drivers use that training)*, parallel park, come to a complete stop at a stop sign rather than slowly rolling through *(like most police cars)*, check the rearview and side mirrors, check the blind spot by actually turning your head to look, the meaning of various road signs, and generally all the "correct" ways to drive.

Because the fairgrounds is relatively flat, he never taught us to take off from a dead start when going up a hill or how to parallel park on a steep incline. Oh, you think starting from a dead stop going up a steep hill is easy? I'm talking about a manual transmission here, not an automatic. If you let the clutch out too fast, the car can lurch forward with one of two things possibly happening: the engine dies or you smash into the car in front of you. Theoretically, both could happen simultaneously. Now if you let the clutch out too slowly, the car tends to roll backwards thus hitting the car directly behind you. It's best not to learn the correct hill clutch-brake technique in real traffic conditions.

But for Dad, all those wonderful driving tips were meant for us and for all other drivers. They did not apply to him. He was prone to speed (even at age ninety-three he was pulled over for going forty-five in a thirty), roll through stop signs, make abrupt lane changes, take turns too fast and too wide, and generally drive aggressively while shouting at other drivers. Over the years I often heard "Get out of the way, Grandpa" even when he himself was in his eighties and nineties. No matter what went wrong out there on the road, it was ALWAYS the other driver's fault. So, as you can imagine, by just riding with him, Jerry and I picked a few driving tips that he failed to mention at the fairgrounds.

In the late fifties and early sixties, you could get a learner's permit at fourteen in Minnesota with just a written test. At fifteen, you could get your permanent driver's license by taking a behind the wheel test. I shall say this once, and then it shall forever be banished to times forgotten: Jerry passed his behind the wheel test on his first attempt. It took me **four times**! Let me just say this in my defense, I didn't steal the folks' car for two years before taking a driver's test (unlike some people I could mention). Anyway, learning to start from a dead stop on a hill and learning to parallel park on a hill when driving a straight stick would have been helpful and beneficial. Also, a tip for young permit drivers, don't speed when taking your driver's test. I've found that as a general rule, testers don't like that. I finally passed by using my dad's car that had an automatic transmission. I got 72 out of 100. Stop laughing—it's a painful memory.

Cars

It was early 1958, and Dad finally bought Mom a new car. By "new," I mean different. It was a two-tone green 1953 Ford four door. It was considerably larger than her old car, the 1946 Ford coupe. That car was given to Jerry who was now sixteen, fully licensed and insured.

Teens loved LOUD cars, but poor Jerry didn't have enough money to buy one of those fancy glass pack mufflers. He decided he'd just have to settle for the next best thing—punching holes in the muffler with an ice pick. Noise was certainly more important than a little carbon monoxide poisoning!

And while it was also popular back then to de-chrome the exterior of the car, it was just the opposite for under the hood: you had to have a chrome air cleaner, generator cover, nut covers for the heads, etc. He spent quite a bit of money on chroming that old flathead V8.

By the time I hit sixteen, the '46 Ford was long gone and Jerry was driving that customized '51 Ford that I mentioned earlier. It was also time for Mom to get a "new" car—and this time she actually did. In the fall of 1961, Dad bought her a brand-new beige Rambler Classic four door. It made those old Nash's look pretty sporty. I inherited Mom's old rusty green 1953 Ford four door. Teens hated FOUR DOORS, but not as much as station wagons!

Shortly before my mother got her new car, I'd use her '53 Ford to take Susie out on Saturday night. It was date night…drive-in movies, drive-in restaurants, cruisin', and maybe just a little parkin' and kissin'.

One Saturday I got up early to wash and wax the car. I had a hot date that evening, so I wanted it to look as good as a rusted green '53 Ford four-door could look. *(Honestly, not too good.)*

After finishing, I drove up to my buddy Frank's house *(yeah, the same place where Jerry had treated me to a death-defying motorcycle ride)*. Being a close friend, he lied and said that the car looked good. We talked a bit, and then I had to head back home to cut the grass and get ready for my date.

A couple things you need to know:

(1) They used to tar streets back then. First, they'd lay down a heavy layer of fresh tar oil, then a dump truck would spread sand all over the top of it. They did all the neighborhood streets. It tended to splatter up black tar onto your car no matter how slowly you drove on it. As I recall, the purpose of tarring streets was to piss people off. So eventually the tar would dissipate but leave behind lots of loose sand—especially at intersections.

(2) Coincidentally, cars built back then did not have positraction rear differential. What? Cars all had rear-wheel drive; and most, until I think 1957, had a locked rear end, meaning that a single axle drove both real wheels in unison rather than independently.

Here is how the combination of (1) and (2) ruined my date: Frank lived on the corner of Arlington and Victoria, and both roads were more widely used than your typical residential side streets. As I left his house, I came to a complete stop at the stop sign (as per the instructions from my father). Then, just for fun, I decided to "lay some rubber." Bad call. I was turning left at the intersection, and my real wheels were both in sand. I gave the car some gas, began turning the steering wheel and then "popped the clutch." Man those rear tires were spinning, squealing, smokin', and spitting up sand until the right rear tire hit dry pavement while the left tire remained spinning in the sand. There was a loud **thunk**, and suddenly I was just coasting. I had snapped the rear axle, and there was no longer any power to either of the rear wheels. I recruited Frank to help me push it the four blocks back home…he from the rear of the car and me from the driver's side. I also had to steer the car through the open driver's side window. We got it back to Orange Ave., which was a hill leading down to Osage and my house. There I hopped in, coasted down, turned left, and came to a stop in front of the house.

"Hey, Dad, something is wrong with Mom's car." A tow truck hauled it away, and my hot Saturday night date was cancelled! Shortly after the Ford was repaired, it was given to me. Any further damage would be at my own expense. Mom got a new beige Rambler out of the deal. UGH.

As soon as school was out for the summer in 1961, I got busy working on the car. Making that four-door Ford look like something was certainly going to be a challenge. The first order of business was to cover up the rusted rocker panels. Easy enough, I'd just buy and install clip-on rocker panels. They probably wouldn't rust out for a couple of years. Next, I wanted to actually customize it.

Bondo is an auto body filler with a consistency similar to peanut butter *(and that plastic wood filler that I used on my models)*. It could be used to repair dents, fill in holes, etc. Just form it, let it dry, sand it, and prime it. I put it to good use, but there was no way that I could re-design a real car as radically as I had my models. It would take WAY too much Bondo to do that. Besides, over time, it cracked.

The 1953 Ford 4-door sedan

I worked on it all summer, and when winter came, I found a double garage to rent in Roseville. It had a wood-burning stove and a whole wall stacked with split logs. The nice couple I was renting from told me I was welcome to use as much wood as I wanted. Having a "heated" garage allowed me to continue the body work throughout the winter months. I didn't mind keeping the car in storage for the winter as I was not allowed to drive it to school anyway. As long as I could use mom's Rambler for dates, I could leave the car in storage and get a lot done on it before spring.

My friend Steve often went with me to work on the Ford. It was a very long and cold walk across the lake and the golf course to get to the rented garage, so thankfully, Jerry stepped up to the plate. He bought us pints of blackberry brandy. Money for the garage rent, the necessary materials for the car, and the brandy came from my part-time job at Country Club Market. I was a carry-out boy, meaning I packed groceries into paper bags for customers, then carried them out to their car. My pay was $1.20 per hour plus tips. A quarter was considered a VERY big deal as most people tipped only a dime.

I finally got the car painted emerald metallic green in the summer of 1962. I had planned on putting a '53 Chev grill in the gaping hole in front, but I just never got around to it.

A Matter of Pride

In the fall, I was getting ready to head back to Cretin for my senior year. Graduation would be in May 1963. I was still working at Country Club Markets but wanted to get transferred from the store near Como to the store near Cretin in Highland Park. That transfer would allow me to put in more hours by working daily right after school. My transfer was denied by one of the two store owners, Bob Naas. Then fate stepped in.

It was a Saturday, and I was working all day at the Como store. It was 10:00 a.m. and time for my fifteen-minute break. I purchased some Twinkies and a bottle of cold Coke and went into the back room of the produce department where I sat on top of a cooler. Bob Naas jumped from store to store around the Twin Cities, and we never knew when he would pop into our store for a visit. But he happened to be on site that particular Saturday morning. He walked into the back room, saw me, saw the Twinkies and the Coke, frowned; and instead of saying, "Good morning, Tom," he said, "Show me the receipt." Not exactly the warm and fuzzy greeting I had hoped to get. Well, it just so happened that I didn't have one because I had walked away before the cashier could hand it to me. He then said, "I don't think you paid for those items."

I had been a loyal employee of Country Club Markets for three years and was more than a little upset at being accused of being a thief. I said, "I did pay for them, Bob." He replied, "I don't believe you."

Blood rushed into my head, and I jumped off the cooler. He quickly backed up, thinking that I was going to attack him (which had actually crossed my mind). I took off my store apron, threw it on the cooler, and said, "I QUIT." I walked out of the store and drove home. I never worked at the Como Country Club Market again.

About noon that day, the phone rang and my mother answered it. She said, "Tom, it's for you." It was Bob Naas. He said, "Tom, I am so sorry. I checked with the cashiers, and Rita said that she had rung up those items for you." I remained silent. I was still so mad that he hadn't trusted me. Then came those magic words: "What can I do to make this right so you will come back to work for us?" My reply: "I want to work at the HIGHLAND store, and I want more hours." He agreed, and I worked there until I graduated.

The Bachmeier Clan

As I mentioned, Susie's dad, Bob, was a very big guy in both height and build. He had been a Navy pilot during WW II, and he could be very confrontational and intimidating. He knew it and relished it. We had not exactly hit it off: First of all, Susie was his and Lila's firstborn, and as such, their "baby." Here I was, a long-haired, duck-tailed Elvis clone dating his little girl. And then there was "the party."

One summer, my folks went out of town for a few days and left Jerry in charge. What could possibly go wrong? Yeah, you can kind of see this one coming, can't you? I thought, *What a great opportunity to throw a party for a few friends.* I assumed that Dad had probably taken inventory of his booze and beer supply before leaving, so once again, it was Jerry to the rescue. While still underage himself, he looked older and had no problem buying the booze and beer for me. We hauled it all down the basement, and then he was off. He had no intention of hanging out at a party with his little brother.

I got everything setup: the bar with liquor and mix, ice, a cooler filled with beer, glasses, snacks, lots of ash trays, and music.

At six thirty I drove over to pick up Susie at her house. Her father gave me strict instructions to have her home by eleven o'clock. It was not a request. Back at the house, guests began arriving shortly before seven o'clock. Maybe twenty in all—mostly couples.

My parents had these little knitted drink glass koozies. Each was a different color with the idea being they'd soak up the glass sweat plus make it easy to identify your glass by the color koozie on it. That evening, many had mixed drinks while others preferred to drink beer out of the bottle. Everybody munched on the chips, bugles, crackers and cheese, and the other snacks while imbibing. Some couples danced while others were deep in conversation. There was a lot of laughter, a little smooching, and maybe a tad too much drinking. All in all, the party seemed to be a success. That is until a buddy and his girlfriend went up the stairs and out the back door. I thought maybe they were leaving early to go "park." Nope—she just wanted to go out where she could throw up. She did that…then she passed out in the back yard. Okay, that was definitely not good, but she seemed to be the exception. Most everyone else was just happily buzzed—and that included Susie.

The "bewitching hour" was approaching, so I began asking folks to head out. God knows I didn't want to get Susie home late. I told her to go straight to bed, and she said that she would. She didn't. She decided it was a good time to set her hair. It wasn't. She began dropping those big curlers on her wood floor and that noise got Daddy's attention in the bedroom next door. He walked into her room, immediately smelled booze on his baby girl's breath, and that was not going to be a good thing for Tom.

The next morning she called and told me what had happened. She warned me not to go to church because Daddy would be looking for me. Hmmm—killed right outside of church…well, it would be convenient for the funeral service. I thought about a last will and testament, but I really didn't have anything except some model cars.

I steered clear of the Bachmeier residence for some time in hopes things would cool off. I fully expected Bob to call my parents, but to best of my knowledge, he never did.

I spent that Sunday cleaning the basement. I hung the dozen or so drink glass koozies on the clothes line in the laundry area to dry; filled bags with napkins, beer bottles, paper plates, butts, and all other signs of a party; and disposed of them in the trash barrels behind Bloom's Market just a few blocks away. I hand washed the snack bowls and platters and put them away, cleaned the tables, wet mopped the floor, and scrubbed the toilet and sink. The place was spotless. Jerry put all the excess beer and booze in his car to take back to his apartment. He even inspected the place and said that nobody would ever know that there had been a party down there. WRONG.

When the folks returned, we implied that we had been angels in their absence. Jerry said that he had stayed at the house, rather than at his apartment, in order to care for his little brother. The truth is, I hadn't even seen him for several days. Nothing new to report Mom and Dad—everything was great. They unpacked, and there was a lot of laundry to do. "Hey, Tom, why are all of these koozies hanging on the line?" Another valuable life lesson learned—the devil is in the details.

Susie's mother, Lila, was an attractive woman who could be the peacemaker in the family. She had a low-key way of calming "Big Bob" down. At the time Susie and I were dating, she was the mother of six children: Susie, Bob, Linda, Jim, Gayle, and Joanie. She seemed to like me, and Susie told me that she had even defended me to Bob. I think she was the reason that I only got a tongue lashing from him rather than beaten to death because of "The Party." I apologized and promised it would never happen again. I was back in the fold—but just barely.

Ahoy

The Bachmeiers had a cabin up on Sugar Lake, which is near St. Cloud. It was shared by a number of relatives who took turns using it for their families. It was an old place with an outhouse—and I hated it. The property was on the north side of the lake, so it did have a beautiful sandy beach. There was a pontoon boat parked at the dock that I found very enticing.

I would be invited on occasion, and almost as soon as I pulled in, Bob would put me to work. I did a lot of things around there from digging plumbing trenches to clearing brush from a back lot. But the rewards were lying in the sun by the beach listening to the waves crash against the shore, boat rides, food off the grill, and, of course, being with Susie.

Now Bob had a unique method of starting the briquettes in the grill… *Gasoline.* I mean any wimp can follow directions and use charcoal lighter fluid. So, as he'd toss a lighted match toward the bowl of gas-soaked charcoal, he'd yell, "Stand back" …then **BOOM**. Flames shot up into the air, and the ground shook. He was delighted. The grilled chicken always had just a hint of 87 octane.

I got along great with Susie's brothers, sisters, aunts, uncles, nieces, nephews, and grandparents. I even got along well with Bob's sister, Jean; her husband; and their kids. Bob's mother, Grace, was more than a little sarcastic and extremely opinionated. She was the one person that Bob did not mess with. His mommy had his number, and I liked her a lot.

In addition to his sister Jean, Bob also had two brothers who lived out of town… Jim in Kansas City and Dick in San Antonio. At first they weren't too sure about me. Who knows what Bob had told them, plus there was something about former military guys vs. long-haired teenagers. But as time went on, we became friends. We often played horseshoes down by the beach at Sugar Lake. All three brothers were VERY competitive and hated to lose. I occasionally won, which I'm sure irritated the hell out of them.

Years later, Susie's uncle Dick had driven up to St. Paul in his newly purchased used motor home. I, along with Bob, Lila, and Susie, was sitting on a lawn chair in the Bachmeier front yard. We were enjoying the weather as well as the lake below when our view was suddenly blocked by a giant bus. As Dick and Chick exited, we all stood to greet them. I asked for a tour, so Dick showed me around. As I walked through, admiring everything, I commented on how much fun it must be to travel this way. His exact words were, "Tom, if you enjoy flushing one hundred dollar bills down a toilet, you should own one."

I loved the Bachmeier clan.

Chapter 3

Chapter 3

Time Flies

Susie and I dated on and off all through high school... I at Cretin; she initially at Archbishop Murray then St. Bernard's. After graduating in 1963, things between us got a lot more serious. I had taken a job as an office clerk/bookkeeper at GTA (full name Farmers Union Grain Terminal Association) in Falcon Heights while she was a telephone operator at NW Bell Telephone in downtown St. Paul.

I was now driving a mint condition 1960 Chevrolet Impala convertible. It was fire-engine red with a white convertible top, and today it would be worth a fortune. I had gotten the car from Jerry, who was getting married and didn't want to be saddled with the payments.

It had the 283-cubic-inch V8 and an automatic transmission. Oh sure, I would have far preferred the more powerful 327 with 4 on the floor, but regardless, it was one good-looking land barge. A porter glass pack muffler gave it that deep throaty sound. You'd rev it up and then let it back down "Baa-room, boom-boom-boom-boom." I so loved that sound. Here are a couple of somewhat painful Impala stories:

Story #1: It was a beautiful warm summer evening in 1963 when I was out just cruising around with the top down. I had already made the various drive-ins: Porky's and Three Bears on University Avenue, Sandy's on Lexington Avenue, and the Roadside in Roseville. It was after ten o'clock, so I decided to head home. As I reached Como Lake, I thought I'd take a quick trip around. The Bachmeier home sat up on a hill overlooking the lake, and Susie's bedroom was in the front on the second floor. Very few homes had air conditioning, so most people had their windows open (including Susie). As I drove on the main road below her home at around 25 mph, I decided to shift into neutral and rev the engine then let it rumble back down. Maybe she'd hear and know it was me driving past. Instead of shifting into neutral, I accidently went right past it and hit reverse. The wheels locked up, the engine died, and the car screeched to a complete stop. *Oh no*, I thought… *This can't be good*. Well, turns out, it wasn't. I shifted into Park, turned the key, and hoped for the best. Whew—at least it started. I then shifted into Drive, and the car began to move forward. Hey, maybe I had dodged a bullet. Nope—it refused to shift out of low gear, so I had to basically crawl back home.

Two repair shops told me that I needed a new transmission, which was very costly. A third shop said, "You only knocked out the universal joints." Thankfully, the repair was not too costly, so the story quickly became somewhat amusing to many—but not so much for me. Really embarrassing.

1960 Chevrolet Impala convertible

Story #2: Shortly after the mis-shift incident, I drove down-town to pick Susie up when her shift at the phone company ended at 10:00 p.m. I parked at the curb on Fourth Street next to Rice Park. The top was down and I sat in the car listening to the radio while I waited. Unbeknown to me, law enforcement was regularly patrolling that area as some sexual activity had been occurring in and around that particular park. A squad car passed slowly by me, and the two uniformed officers took a long look. I figured they were probably just admiring the car and thought nothing of it. A few moments later I heard a husky male voice boom, "What are you doing here?" I looked over, and there were two men standing near the rear of the car just glaring at me. Being a smart-ass teenager, I said, "None of your business." That proved to be the wrong answer. Out came the badges—turns out they were plain-clothes St. Paul cops. "Let me ask you again, what are you doing here?"

No longer cocky, I replied, "Waiting for my girlfriend."

"Let me see your license," one barked.

I took it out, and as I handed it to him, he said, "What's your girlfriend's name?"

"Susie Bachmeier," I nervously replied. "She works at the tele-phone company."

"Uh-huh," he grunted. He handed my license back and asked, "What time does she get off?"

I said, "Ten o'clock."

Both of them instinctively checked their wrist watches in uni-son. It was already a little past—not a good time to be late, Susie! They both just stood there looking at me in silence until she finally emerged from the building and headed toward the car. Seeing her coming, they just walked away. After learning of the sexual activity around the park, I realized that I had been suspected of "being on the prowl."

Susie & me in a photo-booth and our senior year pictures

California

My best friend, Steve McDonough (remember the guy with the Buddy Holly glasses?), well, he and I had planned for nearly a year to take a trip out to California after our graduation. He had gone to Wash (Washington High School on Rice St.). We eventually agreed to go west in January 1964. As that date approached, he began to have some second thoughts and waffle. After the first of the year, he backed out completely. I was pretty annoyed because I wanted to see California in the worst way. So I decided to go anyway—alone. This decision totally freaked the folks out.

It was a typical mid-January day in Minnesota when Mom and Dad dropped me off at the Greyhound Bus Terminal in downtown St. Paul. It was cold, overcast, and dreary. Dirty snow was piled against curbs everywhere you looked. I couldn't wait to escape winter and have some fun in the sun.

My parents had tried everything they could think of to dissuade me from going—including bribery. They were obviously afraid that something bad might happen to me. I admit, I was a little scared myself. This was going to be a very long journey, and I knew that there wouldn't be anybody waiting for me when I arrived in Los Angeles.

The bus wound its way through back roads and little towns until it finally arrived in the big city… Des Moines. A young guy about my age boarded and started down the aisle looking for a seat. He looked at me and decided to take the aisle seat right next to mine. We introduced ourselves, shook hands, and as the miles rolled on and on, we shared our life stories.

Jeff was from a farm family, and he was engaged to be married. No wedding date had yet been set, but plans were in the works. His aunt occasionally visited his family in Iowa, but he had always wanted to visit her in Long Beach. Growing up in such a frigid climate, we had both desired to see the Golden State and walk on its warm sandy beaches.

He told me that January was a good time for him to go as not much was happening on the farm in the dead of winter. He could be spared. I told him all about Susie and how my buddy Steve had backed out of the trip at the last moment. As we rode across the country talking, we decided to share this adventure together.

Before getting off the bus in LA, an unshaven guy with questionable hygiene habits leaned over and whispered, "You can get free food and lodging at the mission." We thanked him for this sage advice and said that we'd give that serious consideration. Hopefully, it wouldn't come to that as we each had cash and travelers checks and, if careful, should be okay.

We got our duffle bags and began walking. We had a city map but no idea where to go. It was mid-afternoon, and we agreed that our first priority was to find a room for the night. As we walked along, we came across an old brick building with a "Rooms for Rent" sign. Inside the small lobby we asked the man behind the registration desk if we could see a room. He looked us over and said, "Follow me." We went up two flights of stairs where he unlocked a room door. I think both of us expected the worst, but to our surprise, it was actually pretty decent. One half of the large room was furnished as a living room with a big sofa, an overstuffed chair, side tables with lamps, a cocktail table, and a portable TV. Large windows overlooked a busy highway eight lanes wide with cars zooming by almost bumper to bumper. It was literally the first time that either of us had seen a freeway. Oh, I had seen the gigantic trench being dug to build one of these high-speed roads between downtown St. Paul and downtown Minneapolis, but I had never seen one completed. It sure looked dangerous to me—cars moving so fast, side by side, and each so close to the one in front of them. I wondered what happened if somebody had to suddenly slam on their brakes.

The other side of the room had two beds, two nightstands with bedside lamps and a doorway leading into a small bathroom. The place was indeed old, but it looked pretty clean, so we rented it for three nights and paid in advance with traveler's checks. We could plan our excursions around LA from here.

We unpacked then wandered over to the windows to watch the cars zip by below. Then looking in the opposite direction, I noticed a small grocery store with a "BEER" sign. I had no idea what the legal drinking age was in California, but assumed it was probably higher than my eighteen years or Jeff's nineteen. Worth a shot. "Want to buy some beer?" I asked. His immediate response was, "Hell, yes." So we walked over to the store, got a six pack out of the cooler, grabbed numerous snacks, and took everything to the register. To our relief, no ID was requested and no questions were asked. We had munchies, we had beer, we had a room, and there was no snow in sight. So far, life in LA was good.

We bummed around downtown, then took a city bus to the beach. It was freezing back in Minnesota and Iowa, but here we were, walking in the sand and watching surfers on this warm, sunny California day. I absolutely loved it and thought, *Maybe I should move here*. After a couple of days "touring" and getting sun-burned, his aunt drove up from Long Beach. She took us back to her home to feed us and to spend the night.

The next morning after breakfast, she drove us over to Disneyland and dropped us off at the main gate. We had both read about and seen this place on TV, but here we were, actually at the entrance to the Magic Kingdom. We were just two overgrown and pretty excited kids. It was such a fun day; we ate, went on rides, ate some more, saw some shows, ate again, more rides, and then we finally collapsed from exhaustion.

Before his aunt was to arrive to pick us up, I decided to have a pastel portrait done by a street artist. It was god awful and didn't look anything like me. How disappointing and what a waste of money.

The next day Jeff and I discussed how to spend the next week. He wanted to stay on at his aunt's place while I wanted to take a bus down to San Diego. We decided to part ways. They agreed to ship my horrible portrait to my house and drove me to the bus station. We said our good-byes and promised to keep in touch—but we didn't. I never saw or heard from Jeff again. At the Greyhound station, I boarded the bus bound for San Diego and once again I was all alone.

Exiting the bus depot, I realized that I had no idea where I was going to go—or how I was going to get there. But, like LA, the weather was warm and sunny; and I knew that I wanted to be near the ocean. With my duffle bag in hand, I began walking with no destination in mind. Then, just up the block, I saw something of interest—a sign that read, "SCOOTERS FOR RENT." Vespa Motor Scooters were parked in front; and they were available by the hour, the day, and the week. No motorcycle license was required—just a valid driver's license. I had one of those. "I'll take one for a week, please," I said.

Now I had never actually ridden a motorized two-wheel vehicle before in my life, but I told them that I was very experienced. In fact, I said that I had one back home. Upon hearing that, they were more than happy to take my money. Now all I had to do was ride out of there without tipping over.

With a map of the area in hand and the duffle bag strapped down behind me, I took off, up the block…and directly onto the **freeway**! I believe the top speed on a Vespa may be thirty-five with some wind at your back, and I was pushing it as hard as I could. Cars zipped by me at fifty-five plus. I still can't believe that I didn't get crushed like a bug. It was frightening, and I was pretty shaken up, so I steered the scooter onto the shoulder of the road where I continued putt-putting along until I reached the first exit.

I had a great time zipping around downtown San Diego and then up to Mission Beach where I got a motel room. There was a nice diner right next door with a pretty darn cute waitress. A California girl to be sure: blond hair, blue eyes, freckles, a deep tan, cute figure, and a nice friendly smile. I sat at the counter, and soon we were talking—then I began to feel guilty. I was madly in love with Susie, but here I was, flirting with this girl, and she was flirting back. Shame on me. I decided to eat future meals elsewhere before I got myself in trouble.

The next morning I hopped on the scooter and drove through Pacific Beach and then up into La Jolla. I assumed that La Jolla meant *paradise* because it was one of the most magnificent places that I had ever seen. I spent the day wandering through the shops and strolling along the palm-tree-lined roads near La Jolla Cove. What a beautiful town. Hmmm—maybe I should move here when I make my first million!

Before leaving, I had to investigate a large cross that I had seen off in the distance. I rode towards it, climbing higher and higher, through a housing development. Upon reaching the summit, I was rewarded with the sight of a huge concrete cross on Mount Soledad. I learned that it had been a San Diego area landmark since 1913. It was magnificent, and I was so glad that I had taken the time to see it.

I spent the next few days wandering around downtown San Diego and its beautiful harbor areas, I then discovered Balboa Park and the San Diego Zoo. I love San Diego and La Jolla, and I have returned a number of times since that first visit.

Oh, I did manage to dump the Vespa once. I was turning right at an intersection and in some sand. I hit the gas too hard causing the rear end to spin left, and over I went. Other than a little embarrassment and scraped up hands and knees, I had no serious injuries. San Diego was the last time that I ever rode a two-wheel vehicle (except for a bicycle).

The trip to California had been fantastic, but my two-week adventure had come to an end. It was time to board the bus back home to winter and to Susie.

Short-Order Cooks

A lot had happened while I was away. Dad had decided to be the financial backer for Jerry's new restaurant venture on Grand Avenue near the corner of Fairview. Both he and Jerry felt that because there were two colleges in the vicinity (St. Thomas and Macalester) a burger-and-malt shop should be popular with students. Plus, the Grandview Movie Theater was just two doors down providing even more customer potential. It would be called… TA-DA…the Golden Grill.

I was unemployed and living at home with the parents. Jerry, his wife Marion, and their baby girl Donna were living in an old apartment on Grand Avenue several doors down from the restaurant location. In discussions with both Dad and Jerry, the idea of me helping open the restaurant came up. I had planned to do a lot of things in my life, but being a short-order cook hadn't been on the list, but I agreed to help out. I'd be paid for my hours worked, providing there was enough money coming in. The game plan was for me to stay on until the Golden Grill was up and operational, then I'd move on.

The restaurant was a Frankenstein—by that I mean the interior came from a number of sources. Virtually everything, including the counter, back bar, grill, booths, and tables had been in other establishments at one time or another. But it all came together and looked good. As Jerry and I were busy setting everything up and cleaning, a guy walked in who looked like he had just come from the set of a gangster movie. "Hi, I'm Al Capone," he said (not really, but I can't recall the guy's name—just the look). "Who's gonna supply the vending machines here?" Funny, we hadn't even thought about any vending machines. He handed us a business card that read something like, "CAPONE ENTERPRISES, Al Capone, President. Slogan: You're going to want to do business with us or increase your insurance coverage."

His company supplied a wide variety of coin-operated machines for the entire Midwest. He strongly suggested that in addition to a jukebox and cigarette machine, that we should also have at least two pinball machines. It was hard to say no to Mr. Capone, but we really didn't have room for the pinball machines, plus we had no desire to become a juvenile delinquent hangout. He looked unhappy at that decision but nodded and continued saying that if we allowed him to furnish the equipment, he'd keep them stocked with fresh packs of cigarettes and the very latest in rock and roll records. In return for granting him this favor, he'd generously give us a 50 percent cut of the profits. The extra income would be nice. It was an offer we couldn't refuse—so we didn't.

The very next day the machines were delivered by Meyer Lansky and Bugsy Siegel (possibly not their real names). One guy handed Jerry a business card. I think under his name was the title of "Enforcer." I think that because he had a little black moustache; a very pocked-marked and scarred face; wore a black shirt, a white tie; and there was a distinctive bulge under his sport coat breast pocket. Great... I suspected that the Golden Grill was now officially in the mob.

After scouting all our competition and getting some advice from the owner of a restaurant near the Minnesota State Capital in St. Paul (Curly Lou's on Rice Street), Jerry signed contracts with various vendors and suppliers, designed the menu, and then had it printed. A lighted "GOLDEN GRILL" sign was hung over the door, and we were set to open. Our specialties:

- The GOLDEN BURGER: two all-beef patties, a three-part bun with the center portion of that bun made into French toast, cheese, onion, lettuce, tomato, pickles, and 1000 Island dressing. 95c /with fries, $1.05. Sound familiar? Except for the French toast part, McDonald's Big Mac, which was introduced in Pittsburgh in 1967 and nationwide in 1968, is quite similar. Trust me, the Golden burger was not only bigger, but considerably better. But then again, look who's rich and who's not!
- The GOLDEN MALT: real hand-scooped vanilla ice cream, milk, orange sherbet, and malt powder: 35c. That was for a full soda glass and the leftover amount still in the mixing can.

Business never really took off like we had hoped. The money that did come in went for supplies, business overhead, and to Jerry. He had a family to support and rent to pay, so he needed the money more than I did. I took virtually nothing out of the business except experience as a fry cook and soda jerk. As Susie and I were getting pretty serious, I felt I needed to start earning some money and saving for our probable marriage.

In May 1964, just three months after joining Jerry at the restaurant, I was back in the grocery store business. I took a job as the accounts payable clerk in the offices of Fairway Foods, another local chain. Jerry ran the Grill for another nine months, but sadly, it closed for good in early 1965.

Pallet Checks

Most of my job at Fairway was to verify that our inventory matched supplier invoices. The loading dock personnel were to compare shipments with invoices, but occasionally there would be discrepancies. When they occurred, I would go into the warehouse and physically count pallets of product. The most common problem was that a partial pallet had been counted as a full pallet or vice-versa. Once everything matched, I approved payment and made sure that we always took the "pay by date" discount (usually 1½ or 2 percent). We never wanted to pay earlier than the due date; conversely, we never wanted to pay late and lose the discount. The job quickly became boring, but on the other hand, the pay was miserable. I knew I couldn't afford to get married working there, so I kept checking the newspaper "Help Wanted" pages for other opportunities.

The '58 Olds

Shortly after leaving the Golden Grill I sold the '60 Chev convertible to pay off my car loan. I had enough money to purchase a neighbor's 1958 Oldsmobile 88. It was a two-door hardtop, and I really liked the looks of the big chrome-laden beast but hated the color. It was a light shade of purple (the official name was Heather) with a white top. I nosed and decked it, fixed the body imperfections with Bondo, sanded the entire car (except the roof), primed the work areas, and had it painted a ruby-red metallic. The front wheel wells were then painted white, and I installed a small light in each so they glowed at night. Some chrome rims and baby moons and the finished product really looked sharp. The neighbor that I had purchased it from walked over one day and kiddingly offered to buy it back.

It was relatively easy to lock your keys inside the car back then, so I decided that wouldn't happen to me—I'd hide a spare door key somewhere on the car. Those little magnetized hide-a-key boxes had a tendency to fall off due to moisture, dirt, and bumpy roads; so I thought I had the foolproof solution… I'd put a key in the engine compartment on that long screw that holds the air cleaner to the carburetor.

One day after work at Fairway, I walked out, started the Olds, and was greeted by some very loud knocking. BANG—BANG—BANG. *YIKES!* My first thought was I must have thrown a rod and the noise was a piston banging against a head. I knew that kind of problem was very expensive to repair. I quickly turned off the engine to prevent any further damage and had a tow truck haul it back to the house.

I knew NOTHING about the mechanical workings of an automobile, after all, I was a "body" guy. My only hope was that one of my more mechanically inclined friends would know how to go about fixing it. I lifted the hood and looked at the big V8 with such a helpless feeling. Then, for some reason, I removed the air cleaner and noticed that the spare key was missing. *"Where on earth could it have gone? Was it possible that the key had broken off and fallen down the carburetor?"*

I decided to start the car to determine which side of the engine the banging was coming from. Once that was determined I removed that head. Unbelievable…lying right on top of a piston was the spare key. The top of it was chewed up, but the rest was still remarkably intact.

I knew that when re-installing the head that the nuts had to be tightened to a certain factory specification. That meant either buying or borrowing a torque wrench. Nobody I knew had one, so I made the purchase. After tightening the nuts, the car ran like a charm. *Interesting side note: it's now fifty-five years later, and I still have that torque wrench. It has been used ONCE.*

1958 Oldsmobile Rocket 88

Chapter 4

Chapter 4

Confrontation

In the fall of 1964 I left my job at Fairway Foods and went to work in the regional offices of Cities Service Oil Company in downtown St. Paul. Once again I was behind a desk punching numbers into an adding machine. It was the same type of work that I had at GTA and Fairway, only it paid more...$300 per month. I needed the extra money because I intended to propose to Susie. In the meantime, Susie had left the phone company for a secretarial position at First National Bank, also downtown.

One evening in November 1964, I did indeed propose. I believe she said yes (it may have been reluctantly—I choose not to recall that). Our parents were well aware of our steady dating since my return from California, but I'm sure they hadn't anticipated our engagement at nineteen years old. We decided to tell her mom and dad first, and I was terrified.

Susie and I sat in the basement rec room of her home trying to figure out how to tell her parents that we wanted to get married. To complicate matters, her mother was pregnant with number 7. Her due date was expected to be in early June. Despite that possible obstacle, we were in love and anxious to start our lives together as soon as possible.

As always, when Susie and I were in her basement together, her mother would peek in (I'm sure at Bob's insistence). That evening when she looked in, Susie said, "Can we talk to both you and Dad?" Her mother's face went from a smile to a very concerned look in an instant. I'm sure her first thought was, "Oh my God, Susie's pregnant too." She wasn't.

Lila disappeared, then returned with Bob. As they walked in, Lila had a weak smile on her face but Bob just glared at me. My heart began pounding, my mouth went dry, and my armpits began to sweat. They sat down, and Susie announced, "We're engaged and plan to get married next year." I think Lila, while surprised, was a little relieved. Bob, not looking at all pleased, asked, "When?" Susie said, "Next year. We could have the wedding in May before the baby is born or in November after the baby is born." At that point Bob rose, turned beet red, and said, "How about a year from November?" Susie and I sat there in silence trying to figure out how to respond. Lila was saying, "Bob, Bob" in an effort to calm him down—but it wasn't working. He was so angry that I thought he might physically attack me.

Her daddy was oh so much bigger than me, but I had had enough. I stood up and went face-to-face with him and said, "We will get married next year."

Had I just actually just done that? He terrified me, but I had lost my cool…and obviously my common sense, but felt I had to stand my ground. Susie began crying and started to leave the room when Lila stopped her just outside the door and told her to get back in and support me. She came back in and said, "Dad, we will get married next year." Nothing more to say—we left. How would my folks react?

My parents were in the den watching TV when we walked in the front door. This time it was my turn to speak up: "Can we talk to you for a minute?" At once, both got that look of concern. The TV was turned off; they got up and came into the living room. We all sat down, and I said almost word for word what Susie had said to her parents: "Engaged, wedding in the next year." My dad, with no anger, just said matter-of-factly, "You're too young to be getting married." Great—no approval there either. Maybe we should just elope. I can't recall how, but eventually the date of May 15 was chosen. Susie and I were happy—the folks, not so much.

My First "New" Car

In early 1965 I decided to shed the 1958 Oldsmobile in favor of something that would be more reliable for a married man and his new wife. I looked at various cars and finally ended up on University Avenue at the Chrysler-Plymouth dealership. All the new '65 models were on display, but there was also a light-blue 1964 Plymouth Savoy two-door coupe on the show floor. I was told that it had been ordered by a 3M executive for his wife, but before taking delivery, he had opted to buy her a more expensive Chrysler. The Plymouth had a manual transmission (which I liked), but only a six-cylinder engine (which I liked less). I paid $1,925 for it, and it also came with that new-car smell!

The Wedding

Much to the chagrin of Jack and Helen and Bob and Lila, Susie and I were married in St. Andrew's Church on Saturday, May 15, 1965. The ceremony was presided over by Father John Fitzpatrick, the assistant pastor. We knew Father Fitz well as he had taught some religion classes at the grade school and had said Sunday mass in the church for many years. He had also been responsible for the Broadway plays that were performed in the church basement. The cast members for the shows were St. Andrew's parish teens, and Susie and I had performed in two of them: *Brigadoon* and *45 Minutes from Broadway*. Father Fitz was also well acquainted with the Bachmeier family and very good friends with my parents. Over the years he had been a guest at many of the parties and social events that included my folks. In fact, Dad would occasionally drop by the rectory to have a drink with Father Fitz. Those visits may also have been to inspect the place to be sure it was being properly maintained. You see, Dad had chaired the fund drive to build that priest's house and devoted countless hours knocking on the doors of parishioners to get pledges. He had also donated considerable money to the cause himself.

As it turned out, the May 15 date was not only unpopular with our parents, but for most attendees as well. Here's why: (1) Minnesota is the "Land of 10,000 Lakes." (2) Those lakes contain fish. (3) Most guys in Minnesota, and a great many gals too, love to fish. (4) May 15 was the fishing opener.

Kidnapped

The wedding had gone well, people threw rice (some too hard), and we were off to the elegant University Club on Summit Avenue. It's interesting to note that our reception was on the very street of mansions where my grandmother had cleaned homes.

I'm sure the reception went well, unfortunately, Susie and I missed most of it. Jerry, and several of my tuxedo-wearing groomsmen, stole the bride. How cute. My buddy, Ted Krammer, said, "Let's go find her." Off we went driving around, aimlessly looking for my bride. Now Ted knew all along where she would be and at what time. He just chose not to share those details with me. This may have been great fun for the groomsmen, but I was getting more and more agitated by the minute. This was not how I had envisioned spending my wedding day.

We finally pulled into the A & W Drive-in on Como Avenue near Snelling (across from the state fairgrounds). Over the years Susie and I had gone there many times. Besides having great root beer, they had a "family" of burgers: the baby burger (a single), the mama burger (a double), and the papa burger (a bigger double).

Oh, you probably don't care about that, you want to know if my bride was there. She was, and in fact she was eating some fries when we pulled alongside. She looked over and smiled, apparently not too upset about being kidnapped. Understandable—the fries were quite good.

Back at the reception, we arrived in time to cut the cake, dance, mingle a bit, and then Susie tossed the bouquet. Then people began leaving…probably in a hurry to bait their hooks.

The Honeymoon

For some reason that escapes me, we decided to drive first to Denver, then onto the Black Hills for our honeymoon. We were on a two-lane highway in the middle of a farm field when I decided to "try out" the new car. I had it up to ninety when a highway patrol car passed from the opposite direction. C'mon, what are the odds? I looked in the rearview mirror and saw his brake lights, then his car spun a U-turn and lit up with flashing red lights. By now I had slowed to the posted speed limit—as if that would do any good.

I pulled to the side of the road and nervously waited for him. Susie, by the way, was laughing. He got out, put on his trooper hat, then walked up to my open car window.

"Do you know how fast you were going?" he asked.

My first thought was, *Maybe he hadn't clocked me and doesn't know my exact speed.* I said, "The speed limit, sir."

That did not please him. "No, I'm sure it was considerably more than that."

Just keep your mouth shut, I thought.

He held out his hand and said, "Driver's license, please."

I dug it out of my wallet and handed it to him.

As he studied it, he asked, "Where you heading?"

"We're on our honeymoon and going to Denver," I replied.

He seemed to mull that over for a moment, then bent down and looked in at Susie. Thankfully, she had stopped laughing.

"I'm going to let you off with a warning this time, but you better slow down."

"Yes, sir."

We were once again on our way to the mountains.

We stayed downtown Denver at a Hilton that had a beautiful restaurant on the top floor. We were seated by the large windows that overlooked the city with a backdrop of spectacular mountains. Susie suggested that we order a glass of wine, but I was afraid of being embarrassed if the waiter asked for ID. He didn't. We took in the breathtaking vista sipping on merlot. After a wonderful steak dinner, we went back to our room. Our son Mike was born nine months later.

Frightening

Despite being mid-May, the snow in the mountains was still very deep. The roads were clear, but the walls of snow on each side must have been eight feet high. It was like driving in a tunnel. We toured the area for a couple of days, and then we were off to Rapid City, South Dakota, and Mount Rushmore. Nothing more romantic than four dead presidents.

It was early afternoon when we pulled into the parking lot at Terry Peak. The skiing season was over, but the chair lift was still operating for those wanting a ride to the mountain top. We purchased our lift tickets and then climbed into one of the swinging lift chairs. It was bright, sunny, and around seventy; yet there was still considerable snow on the ground. We got off at the summit and marveled at the views but noticed that the temperature had dropped considerably. We had only light jackets with us, and they were not nearly warm enough. Then some very ominous black clouds began to move in quickly. We could see lightning bolts flashing down as they approached, and we were told to get back on the lift immediately for a ride back to the base. We didn't make it.

It began to rain hard—and it was a VERY COLD rain. The temperature must have plunged thirty degrees in a matter of minutes, and we were both wet and freezing. Lightning flashed everywhere, and we thought that if lightning struck the overhead metal cables, we'd die. The chair lift suddenly jerked to a halt. There was complete silence as the wind swung us back and forth over the snowy mountain some thirty feet below.

It seemed like an eternity before two men appeared.

One hollered, "Drop that thin rope under your seat."

I reached down and found it and realized that one end was tied to the seat bar.

"Don't untie it," he hollered. "Just drop it as it is."

It was long enough to reach him, and he tied it to a much thicker rope with a loop on the end of it. "Pull it up."

I did, and then he said, "Put the loop over your head and then under your arms, climb over the rail, and slowly let go. We're going to lower you down."

ARE YOU SHITTIN' ME?

"It's the only way down," he said.

Susie went down first; and I pulled the rope back up, looped it under my arms, and was lowered. We stood there in the snow with rain pouring down on us. As they began walking to the next chair, one yelled over his shoulder, "You'll have to walk down." Well, we were at least back on solid ground.

It was a long way down the steep mountain, trudging through the snow that at times was over a foot deep. Our tennis shoes were not exactly made for this. When we finally reached the base, we were both shivering violently and our teeth were chattering. I don't think either of us had ever been that cold—and we were from Minnesota! We had no dry clothes with us—everything was back at the motel. We drank hot chocolate and hot coffee, but neither warmed us much. There were a lot of wet, cold people like us milling around, and everybody seemed to be in shock. I finally said, "Let's go—we can turn the heater in the car on full blast on the way back to the motel."

Back in our room we stripped off our wet clothes, and Susie headed into the bathroom for a hot shower. I toweled off and dove under the covers. It took a very long time to warm up. Cuddling helped.

Home Sweet... Bang, Bang, Bang

Our first home together was the upstairs of an old white house at 1054 Forest (on the corner of Forest Street North and Cook Avenue East). That's on St. Paul's eastside, and it was a predominantly Polish neighborhood. Our landlords were the Luekeseski's, an older couple who owned the home and lived on the main floor. As part of our $75 monthly rent, we had the use of the freestanding garage as they no longer owned a car. Susie continued to work at First National Bank. As she did not drive at the time, she would ride back and forth with me as I also worked downtown and had similar hours.

Susie had been having a lot of morning sickness, so at seven months we decided it might be best if she quit work and stayed home. If she wanted to go somewhere, she could ride the city bus. There was a bus stop directly across the street from the house in front of a small neighborhood grocery store. We frequented that store a lot *(we practically lived on boxes of Kraft mac and cheese)* because the owner would hold our personal checks until payday. He did that voluntarily after learning that trying to cash them any sooner caused them to bounce. About two blocks up was St. Casimir's Catholic Church. We usually walked to church each Sunday.

The Luekeseskis were very noise conscious. They could hear a pin drop upstairs and would continually bang a broom handle against their kitchen ceiling to let us know that we were making too much noise. Our breathing was too much noise. I imagined that their kitchen ceiling must be full of broom-handle indentations.

Coincidence

Susie's mother Lila, gave birth to her seventh child on June 5, 1965—just three weeks after our wedding. Susie, who was Bob and Lila's first child, had been born on June 5, 1945. Richard (everybody called him Dickie) and Susie were BOOKENDS. They were born exactly twenty years apart.

A New Job

I was tired of sitting behind a desk, so one day I went into the sales manager's office and asked if I could get into sales. The little punk actually smirked at me and said that only EXPERIENCED salespeople could work for him. As I had no sales experience, this looked like a dead end. Besides, I no longer wanted to work for that smart-ass. I went home and told Susie how disappointed I was and that I just had to find a job where I wouldn't be tied to a desk and adding machine all day. A couple of days later she handed me that afternoon's *St. Paul Dispatch* with a "Help Wanted" ad circled. The ad was actually from the *St. Paul Dispatch* (PM paper) and *Pioneer Press* (AM paper), and it said they were looking for an outside classified advertising salesman. (Yes, sales**man**. Everybody discriminated back then). It said that sales experience was preferred. She encouraged me to apply, so the very next day, I walked down to the newspaper building and filled out an application. I was then taken to the office of John Henry, the recently named classified advertising manager. He was looking to make his very first hire.

He looked over my application and then politely explained that he preferred somebody with sales experience. I told him how much I needed somebody to give me a chance to prove myself.

He said, "Okay, look, I'm going to have you take a sales aptitude test. That will tell us if you have any instinctive sales ability without actually having any experience." I quickly agreed to take it.

The test indicated that I had zero sales knowledge. Big surprise—I was a bookkeeper. After reviewing the results, John said that he was sorry but he wasn't interested in hiring me. The next day I called him and told him of my continued interest and begged him to give me a chance. Nope. The next day I called him again, and we went through the same thing. I continued to call him every day for a week, and then I mailed him a letter requesting another interview. His secretary called one day and said, "Mr. Henry, would like to see you."

Once again I sat in front of John, and the poor guy looked exasperated. "Look, Tom," he said, "you're a very persistent young man, but I really need somebody with experience. Even the aptitude test indicated that you are probably not cut out for sales."

I pleaded with him: "Please give me a chance, John. If I don't work out within a reasonable period of time, fire me. At least we can say we both tried—and I promise I'll stop bugging you." He let out a deep sigh…then made me his very first hire. I had a new job paying $97.50 per week, which was a big increase over my Cities Service salary. Remember that persistence lesson that I had learned at the monument company? Well, it had just worked again.

And Baby Makes Three

In February 1966, we welcomed our firstborn. The doctor had been telling us for months that based on the baby's heart rate, we were going to have a girl. That being the case, we decided on the drive down to St. Joseph's Hospital for delivery to name her Michelle. HA… Michelle became Michael John.

Poor little Michael had the croup and an ear infection, so he cried a lot. We had to keep a steamer going for him to relieve some of his congestion. Well, apparently the noise coming from upstairs upset the Luekeseski's to no end. The broom-handle banging was almost continuous. In March, we received a registered letter informing us that we were being evicted effective May 1.

Dad to the Rescue

We immediately began looking for a new place to rent. My dad suggested that we buy a house instead, but as we were down to one income and had no savings, that looked impossible. He then agreed to make our down payment providing we re-paid him.

We found a nice two-story house with white wooden siding on Ashland Ave. It was in a beautiful old neighborhood with large mature trees on each side of the street. The asking price was $14,500, and it was the one we wanted. All of the paperwork at the bank and the real estate office was signed with Dad co-signing everything. He had to because we were only twenty and not of legal age. Our $75 monthly rent had become a $104 house payment—but that included principle, interest, taxes, and insurance. *Mostly interest.* The home had been owned for forty years by an elderly couple named Smith. They were only the second owners of the house, now Susie and I were the third. Isn't that amazing? A seventy-eight-year-old house and we were just the third occupants. I began scraping and re-painting the peeling exterior that very summer.

1188 Ashland Avenue, St Paul, MN

A Growing Family

In September 1967, our second son, Robert Thomas, was born. The doctor had told us all along that we would be having another boy. This time he had actually been correct. Great…he could wear Mike's hand-me-downs. We were living from pay check to pay check, and on the weekends we'd actually drink Thunderbird or Blue Nun wine because it was so cheap. With two children and a house payment, it was increasingly important I move ahead in my career and generate more income. I was motivated.

Advertising sales positions at the newspaper were covered by a union called the Newspaper Guild. There was a guaranteed salary increase on each anniversary date for six years. Sixth-year scale was "top scale." Management could give you "merit pay" over scale if they felt that you deserved it. There was also an opportunity to earn some limited commissions or incentive prizes from various sales contests. I had survived the probationary period and moved to second-year scale in February. I was proving to John that he had been right in hiring me. I continued to call on very small classified contract advertisers located in downtown St. Paul. I mainly picked up ads and brought them back in for processing. Not much actual "selling" involved, but I was soaking up sales techniques by observing and listening to the experienced sales reps who handled larger accounts such as auto dealers and the real estate companies. I was also learning valuable interpersonal and customer relations skills from the accounts that I was responsible for. I read books on successful salesmanship as well as motivational materials. I had even attended a Dale Carnegie course shortly before leaving Cities Service. I was a sponge, and this education would later pay big dividends.

A Mentor and a Friend

Susie's dad and I were getting along a little better now that I was a responsible husband, father, and homeowner. He had an old friend named Jack Moser who worked at the newspaper in the promotions department. I had met Jack early on in my employment at the paper and loved his sense of humor and especially his laugh. I was only twenty-one and he in his mid-forties, but for some reason, we just clicked. I constantly made fun of his "old age." Many years later, Jack, his wife Diane, Susie and I were with a newspaper group on a trip to Cancun. There was a one-day trip to Chichen Itza— the Mayan ruins that was a two-and-a-half-hour, 112-mile trek on a bouncing old bus. When we finally arrived and got off the bus, I said to Jack, "Well, does it look any different from the grand opening ribbon cutting ceremony?" That good-natured jabbing continued for forty years.

Jack was a master wordsmith and could make anything sound great. His creative skills and copywriting abilities eventually led to a new *Creative Services Department*, which he managed. After consultation with the sales rep regarding a specific account, he would prepare an ad concept, a rough ad layout, the headline, and the copy. Once approved, it was assigned to a graphic artist for completion. All the creative work, with the exception of finished art charges, was free to our advertisers. I spent a lot of time with Jack utilizing his talents for my clients every chance that I got. And I learned.

Not the Big Deal

In 1968, Monty Hall brought his TV Show *Let's Make a Deal* to the St. Paul auditorium. Susie and her friend Bev couldn't resist dressing up and going. They were both chosen from the huge crowd waiting outside to be part of the studio audience. Susie, wearing my old Cretin High School US Army hat and jacket, was chosen to come up and make a deal. She choose a curtain and won a Wurlitzer console stereo valued at $500 plus $250 worth of Shakey's pizza. While that sounds like a $750 deal, in reality, it wasn't. The $500 stereo value was the manufacturer's suggested retail price and nobody paid that. The $250 pizza deal actually expired in just ninety days. The average price for a whole pizza back then was around $2.50, so $250 worth of pizza was a lot to eat in three months. We did put a number of them in the freezer, but they never tasted as good as fresh. As I had failed to include the prizes on my tax return, my H&R Block tax preparer, Art Olsen, had to explain all this to an IRS agent when we were later audited.

The Magnavox was truly awesome. It was six feet of gorgeous Cherrywood cabinetry, and it contained a turntable, an AM/FM radio tuner, woofers, I'm guessing some tweeters, plus lots of record album storage. It was really a source of pride because most people couldn't afford to purchase one like that. It sold for four times our monthly house payment!

Even though the free pizza deal was over, we continued to eat Shakey's Pizza. With a one year old and a two year old, we found that it was usually best to pick it up and eat it at home. Later, as the kids got older, we'd actually dine-in. They loved to stand on the little elevated wooden walkway and look through the big plate glass windows into the kitchen and watch as pizzas were being made.

Little Darling

Mike, being the oldest, was the first to get into trouble. One fine summer Saturday afternoon, when he was about two and a half, Mrs. Diamond, our next-door neighbor, knocked on our front door. Susie and I both answered, and Mrs. Diamond asked, "Do you know where your son Mike is?"

Well, that seemed like an odd question!

"Sure," Susie said. "He's upstairs taking a nap."

"No," came her reply. "He's out on the roof."

WHAT?

"Come, see," she said.

So we all went out and slowly peered around the side of the house and nearly fainted. On the roof, over the bay windows that protruded from the dining room, was little Mike. The roof had a steep pitch and measured only about four feet from the side of the house to the gutter. There he sat, right at the very edge, with a drop of about twelve feet.

Mike's bedroom, which was directly above the dining room, had just one double-hung window. As it was a warm summer day, the window was open (the bottom half slid up). There was a screen on the outside of the window, which hooked shut at the bottom from the inside. Mike had un-hooked the screen, crawled out onto the roof, and the screen, then closed behind him.

My first thought was, *Ladder*, but I was afraid that might take too long. I raced back inside, up the stairs and into his room. I did not want to frighten him, so I walked over to the window and said, "Hi, Mike." His head turned, and he said, "Hi, Daddy." I didn't think that I could open the screen very far without bumping into him. I was also fearful that he'd try to stand up to get out of the way if I pushed it too close to him. I said, "Sit tight, Mike. I'm going to open the screen as far as I can. But I don't want you to move, okay?" He just smiled and said, "Okay." He apparently had no fear of heights. I'm not sure if that's a good or a bad thing.

Susie and Mrs. Diamond, an elderly woman, stood below looking up. If Mike fell, Susie would have to try to catch him or, at least, break his fall. My heart was pounding, and my hands were sweating profusely as I slowly pushed the screen open. There was just enough room for me to squeeze partially out and extend my arm. "Grab onto my hand," I said. He reached for my hand, and I was able to grip his arm. I said, "Don't stand up, Mike, just crawl over here to me." He smiled and did as he was told. I got an arm around him, moved him off to the side so I could open the screen further, and then lifted him back inside.

That very afternoon I put a ladder up and secured the screen so that it could no longer be pushed outwardly again—even if un-hooked. Once was more than enough.

Think I'm done? HA. About a year later, also on a sunny summer Saturday, Mr. Diamond knocked on our back door. He explained that he had been painting some lower boards on the outside of his house. Mike had been watching for a while but left before Mr. Diamond had decided to take a short break and go inside for something to drink. When he came back out, the paint can and the brush were gone. He suspected that Mike may have been involved. The paint thief had escaped but left a clear trail behind…the sidewalk leading from the back of Diamond's house to the garage and alley was painted white.

I called Mike's name but got no response. We looked inside Diamond's garage, but he was not in there. We continued down the alley and then spotted an open garage door a few homes down. And there, inside that garage, was Mike, with the paint can and the brush. He was busy painting an aluminum fishing boat.

Moving On

I had made it to the fourth year pay scale, and consequently we were doing much better financially. I had recently accepted a new sales position in the retail advertising department due to my good work in classified. I was doing well, and I think John was very proud of me.

The year 1970 turned out to be a big year: new job, new house, new car(s), and a new baby. In June, our third child was born—Thomas Richard Jr. We now had three boys. What could possibly go wrong?

Me, Bob, Tom, Jr., Mike, Susie, 1970

We sold the house on Ashland for $15,900 and moved into 3394 Richmond Ave. It was a one-year-old rambler (single-story home) on a large corner lot in the St. Paul suburb of Shoreview. It was small, about 1200 square feet, but had an attached double garage and a full unfinished basement. The price was $28,000.

The couple who had originally purchased the home from the builder could no longer afford the monthly payments.

The yard was a blank slate—nothing but grass around the entire house. No trees, no bushes, no shrubs, no flowers, no fence, no patio or deck—just grass. I hated the color of the siding—it was a pale baby blue, and I was determined to change that as soon as possible.

In the fall, I traded the '64 Plymouth in on a new 1971 Chevrolet Malibu with an automatic transmission. Susie wanted to get her driver's license, so this new car was perfect for teaching her. Once she got her license, I bought her a car from Larry Otte, a fellow sales rep at the paper. Funny story about Larry: Nearly everyone in the ad department smoked, but Larry was one of only two guys who smoked a pipe. We noticed that he always left his pipe and tobacco pouch on the top of his desk when he went somewhere—like the bathroom. As we all hated the smell of the cheap tobacco that he used, we hatched a plan to encourage him to switch. An un-named person chopped up some rubber bands and waited for him to make a potty run. When he did, the chopped up rubber was mixed in with his pipe tobacco. He came back, filled his pipe, and, unfortunately, never noticed the difference. (Yes, I chopped up the rubber bands.) Oh, Susie's car… it was a yellow 1965 Mercury Montery two-door hardtop with black leather interior and a black vinyl roof. It was pretty good-looking and in perfect condition. Susie called it the Bumble Bee, and now she had the freedom to travel about at will.

Hey, Bartender

If you ever watched the TV show *Mad Men*, you have some idea about the over imbibing that took place at lunch in the sixties and even into the seventies. We'd often take customers out to lunch and occasionally not eat. Russ Schwab, a senior sales rep, once told me that when he interviewed at the paper years before, one of the questions was, "Can you hold your liquor?"

I recall one "no food" lunch at the Coachman on Maryland Ave. and Dale St. My boss, Gordy Fay, and I were trying to convince a grocery store owner/operator to spend more ad dollars in our newspaper. This was not an easy task. The stores were named Wild Bill Knowlan's. Bill was a heavy set, jovial guy, and I do believe the term "wild" accurately described him.

We were seated at a table talking when he suddenly jumped up and began handing out some kind of trinket with his store logo on it to each and every patron. When he returned, another round of drinks was ordered, we'd talk, and off he'd go again handing out something different. This continued until shortly after 2:00 p.m. It was painfully obvious that there would be no actual business transacted that day. We left—Bill stayed.

On another occasion, we were going to make a luncheon presentation to the general manager and the promotion manager of Har Mar Mall in Roseville. They chose the restaurant—the Continental Room at McGuire's Hotel in Arden Hills. It was an upscale restaurant and quite popular for business luncheons. Gordy and I had ridden together and arrived early. After being seated, he suggested that we order a drink. I ordered a perfect brandy Manhattan (brandy over ice, a dash of sweet vermouth, a dash of dry vermouth, and a couple of olives). We were just finishing our drinks when the promotion manager arrived and said that the GM might be late. "Let's have a drink," he said. Another Manhattan. Then the GM arrived. He wanted to have a drink before eating. Manhattan number 3. I had skipped the most important meal of the day and was now toasted. I recall eating a Monte Cristo sandwich, but little else.

When we walked out the door I told Gordy that I didn't want to go back to the office feeling so tipsy. Thankfully, I lived only a few blocks away, so he dropped me off at home. Susie was not impressed with my condition. I promised myself right then and there that I would never over indulge at lunch again…and I never did. It might have been common place, but it was unprofessional and could certainly be dangerous if driving were involved.

We often had customers come down to the paper for research presentations. We conducted market studies; and the results indicated where, and from whom, people bought various products and services. This was of great interest to our advertisers as it showed their market share and where they had opportunities to grow.

These presentations were usually in our advertising conference room and shown after cocktails and lunch. I was the designated bartender. Bloody Marys were always the favorite, but we had a complete bar setup. I pretended to drink, but my glass contained only the mix—a virgin Mary. Some customers actually ordered several drinks at once so they wouldn't run out during the presentation! I witnessed several customers doze off when the lights went out for the slide show. But booze wasn't the only sleep aid:

We were in the conference room at Midway Shopping Center, and our presentation was a demographic research study showing various shopping center and mall rankings in multiple business categories. It was unusual for the ad director to attend one of these, but George McFadden had insisted on being there. He had his pilot's license and owned, along with another guy, a small airplane kept at an airport near Stillwater. Several times a week, depending on weather conditions, George would get up very early, drive down to Stillwater, and fly his airplane before coming into work. He apparently had been out flying on that particular day because when the lights went out, so did he…and he snored!

Dirty Work

The yard wasn't quite as bare anymore. I had planted a lot of trees, as well as numerous shrubs and bushes, around the house.

Several people donated to the cause: a guy on my bowling team gave us some little pine trees; and my aunt Helen and uncle Bob brought over some peony bushes, rhubarb, and a couple of bags of cow manure. Uncle Bob had access to a lot of cow manure as he worked at the South St. Paul stockyards. Our corner lot was very large, and it easily absorbed many small plantings. Budget was a serious consideration—and as LITTLE trees and shrubs were considerably less expensive than BIG ones, we decided to be both frugal AND patient knowing that everything would eventually grow up and fill in.

Gone

Labor Day had been on Monday, September 6, in 1971, and the three-day weekend weather was perfect. I had decided to take several additional days off work to complete a new patio in our backyard. I got up early Tuesday morning and headed out to get as much done before it got too hot. Music played from the radio plugged into the garage wall outlet. Yeah, I was still listening to TOP 40 stuff.

A little over a mile straight north of our house was Interstate 694, and just beyond that, they were building a staggeringly tall TV tower. Upon completion it would rise 1,466 feet. We watched for many months as it went up and marveled at the immense size. Now nearly complete, it needed only some large metal pieces to be hoisted up to complete a triangular candelabra platform near the top. That platform would hold ten smaller antennas.

To give you some height perspective, the Statue of Liberty is 305 feet tall from her base and foundation to the top of her torch; the Eiffel Tower is 1,063 feet tall from its base to its tip, and the Empire State Building is 1,450 feet tall from sidewalk to tip. At 1,466 feet, the top half of the tower could easily be seen from our back yard. Hills, homes, and trees blocked our view of the lower half.

Shortly before 10:00 a.m. on Tuesday, September 7, 1971, our next door neighbor, Carol, walked over and asked, "Where did the TV Tower go?" I looked over and sure enough, it had totally disappeared. We both just stood there in silence looking at the sky where it had been trying to comprehend what had happened. Then they began…more sirens than I had ever heard before in my life. It was eerie. They were coming from all directions. A few moments later came the loud thumping of helicopter blades.

I raced into the house, turned on the TV, and yelled to Susie that something had happened to the TV Tower. Mike (five and a half) and Bob (four) ran in through the front door. They had just witnessed the tower disappear from the horizon while playing across the street with their friend Billy Merrill.

Channels 4 (WCCO) and channel 11 (WTCN) were off the air. Both stations had earlier elected to move their operations from the Foshay Tower in downtown Minneapolis to temporary antennas in Shoreview. Channels 2 (KTCI), channel 5 (KSTP), and channel 9 (KMSP), who hadn't yet moved their operations, were still broadcasting. We stood there in the living room, flipping from station to station until we finally saw what we had been searching for.

BULLETIN: *"It has just been reported that the TV Tower being constructed in Shoreview has collapsed. Many are feared dead and injured. More details as they become available."* The details were awful. Over one thousand tons of metal had crashed down in just fifteen seconds. Live helicopter shots showed the twisted metal and snapped tower cables lying on the ground. There were seven confirmed dead and many injured. For me, it was one of those "where were you when" moments.

The tower collapse was caused by faulty welds according to the Minnesota Department of Labor and Industry. A separate engineering study, however, indicated that several problems most likely contributed: faulty welds done off site, several steel sections not fully bolted, and a weight imbalance on the triangular platform.

Three separate 1,400 foot towers later replaced the single fallen one. No triangular platforms were used on any of them.

Valuable Lessons

I quickly realized that most ad department managers had been, or currently were, involved in civic organizations. As we lived in the suburb of Shoreview, I had chosen to work with the Shoreview Jaycees on various events. Our largest project was the annual Shoreview Festival at Island Lake Park. There were lots of food booths, games for the kids, arts and crafts, and the big attraction…the Bald Eagle Water Ski Club. They performed around the Twin Cities area but regularly practiced right there at Island Lake. For that reason they kept a large ramp anchored in the middle of the lake all summer long. For our big festival, they would put on a water skiing exhibition that included lots of ramp jumping. All this was well and good, but it was not visible to the top execs at the newspaper. I knew I had to get involved with **St. Paul** projects.

In late summer a bulletin came out requesting volunteers to be "advisors" for Junior Achievement. I was the only person who signed up from advertising, but there were three others from other departments who also signed up. Four advisors was just the right number. We would teach a group of high school students one evening a week about business: choosing a product, manufacturing that product, pricing and marketing, techniques for door-to-door sales, accounting, etc.

JA was a pet project of our publisher, Tom Carlin. He met with the four of us and thanked us for volunteering. He told us that the newspaper would cover the cost of a nice dinner each week prior to our JA meetings. We decided we wanted to eat dinner each week at the Whiskey a-go-go. They had great T-bone steaks. I talked to the manager there, and he agreed to invoice Tom Carlin at the paper on a monthly basis. Week one we ate, did JA, then we all went home. Week two was pretty much the same, but we discussed the possibility of getting together afterwards for a drink or two. Week three we ate, told them to keep the tab open, did JA, then went back to drink. In fact, we had several drinks. It was the same for week four…and then I got a call from Tom Carlin!

As I entered the publisher's office, he got up, came out from behind his desk, and motioned for me to sit on the sofa. He sat down next to me. He wanted a JA update report, which I gladly gave him. It was all positive stuff. Then he said that he had a couple of questions regarding the Whiskey a-go-go invoice he had just received. I squirmed a little and immediately got defensive: "We get together afterwards to discuss the JA meeting and then make plans for our next meeting." He smiled and nodded as if to say "Bullshit" but in a nice way. "Tom, I know you can't have a drink before JA, so I don't mind that you have a drink afterwards. Now here's the deal, I'll keep paying for your steak dinners and for ONE after-meeting drink, but any more than one drink will be out of your own pockets. Please inform the other three advisors." I agreed. He smiled. As we stood, he shook my hand and once again thanked me for volunteering. The meeting was over.

Two things struck me that lasted for the rest of my career: (1) Never keep a desk between you and an office guest *(unless your objective is to intimidate them)*. As my career progressed, I always made it a point to get up and come around to meet everyone who entered my office. For discussions and meetings, we'd most often sit at a small round conference table. (2) You can chastise an employee without destroying them. Leave them some dignity and you'll get better performance as well as their loyalty and respect. Tom Carlin taught me all that in one short meeting.

Water, Anyone?

My pal from work, Jack Moser, lived just a few blocks away. We'd often ride to work together and laugh most of the way in each direction. No matter how rotten a day had been, our rides together were guaranteed to brighten it.

Jack was driving his little VW bug, and I was in the passenger seat. We were on Cannon Ave. approaching the rear of my house, and as we got closer, we both saw a most unusual sight at the very same time: there was my youngest, two-year-old Tommy, standing by an open basement window holding the garden hose. That hose was indeed turned on, and he was apparently trying to turn the basement into an indoor swimming pool. Jack laughed, and I finally uttered the first thing that popped into my mind: "Isn't that cute?" When I said that, Jack just exploded in laughter. As I mentioned before, he had the most wonderful laugh. If you were anywhere in the area when Jack laughed, you also had to laugh. It was just that contagious.

Over the years, he often reminded me of my freakishly calm reaction: "Isn't that cute?"

Neighbors

Nearly all our neighbors were young couples with small children. As there were no fences around any of the yards, we looked down an entire block of back yards from our patio. That was both good and bad...bad if you wanted privacy, good if you were in the mood to socialize. If you were seen out on your patio or in your yard, people would sometimes just wander over. You couldn't be rude, so you'd say, "Would you like a drink?" Most of the time they'd say yes. There were many Saturday nights during the summer when somebody on the block was hosting a patio party. They were always great fun, but there was way too much drinking. Sunday mornings could be painful.

Tom Jr., Mike & Bob in the sandbox in Shoreview, 1972

I had built our patio using pavers that were given to me by Frank and Judy, the neighbors in back of us. They had decided to have cement instead of pavers. After we hauled all the pavers from his yard over to ours, he went back home to tear up the area, remove grass and dirt, and then frame it in for the concrete pour. A big job to be sure. He had spray painted an outline of the new patio and then begun to follow that paint line with the power tiller he had rented. The tiller tore up the grass with ease, and it dug down deep to churn up the dirt. All was going well until he severed the natural gas line leading to his outdoor grill. He managed to find the shut off valve before the whole neighborhood exploded. Next, he cut through the electrical line that powered his patio lamppost. Not to be deterred, he continued on until he chopped up the underground telephone line leading to his house. The poor guy was a little despondent when he walked over and asked to use our phone. An expensive patio to be sure!

Frank owned an office supply company, and his business was thriving. One evening I was out cutting the lawn, and when I got to the back yard, I had to stop and laugh out loud...there was Frank, a big grin on his face, cruising around his back yard on a new riding mower. He had one hand on the steering wheel and the other was raised triumphantly in the air clutching a cocktail. Fun times (but tough on the liver).

Chapter 5

Chapter 5

My Career

It was 1976, and as I celebrated my tenth anniversary at the paper, everything was going quite well. I had developed into one of the top salespeople in the advertising division in terms of exceeding sales quotas, account growth, and revenue gains. I frequently came in number 1 in various contests such as new contracts and special section ad sales. I had even won a new RCA color television set. Over the years I had been promoted to ever-increasing sales territory responsibilities with larger and more important accounts. I was compensated accordingly with additional merit pay over union scale. Here are a few of my assignments:

In January 1971, I became the advertising manager for the newspaper's Sunday rotogravure magazine called *CAPITAL*. I loved that job as it felt like I was running my own little business… I was a team of one. I had to sell and produce all the magazine's local advertising. I had re-designed all of the sales collateral, marketing materials, rate structures, and even the promotional ads. I was making some progress in securing new advertisers—but it was a tough sell and an uphill battle. We were still a letterpress newspaper, and the color ad reproduction on newsprint was not good. The main benefit of the Sunday roto magazine was that it offered spectacular color—but at a high cost.

I had been reading that many newspapers across the country were discontinuing their Sunday magazines as they were no longer profitable. There were four contributing factors for that: (1) national brand advertising had moved away from local magazines and into multi-market Sunday magazines like *Parade* or free-standing inserts, (2) the long lead copy deadline-ad materials had to be in house nearly a month prior to publication, (3) the high cost of printing the magazines outside on special rotogravure presses (our magazine was printed in Cleveland), (4) the necessary high ad costs charged to offset the printing and shipping expenses.

One afternoon I returned to the office and found out that a decision had been made to kill our magazine. I was devastated. I had worked so hard to turn it around, but it was nearly impossible to sell enough new local advertising to offset the high production costs. Bye, bye, *CAPITAL*.

So with the demise of the magazine in August 1971, I was named department store advertising manager. That meant that I was responsible for the sales and service of our biggest revenue-producing customers: local department store chains *Dayton's, Donaldson's, Power's, and Field-Schlick*; national chains such as *Montgomery Ward, Sears, and JC Penney*; and discount stores *K-Mart* and *Target* (WalMart was not even on the radar yet in our market).

In February 1974, I was given the additional responsibilities for all shopping center and mall advertising.

Then, in December 1974, I was named to a true "management" position: assistant classified advertising manager. John Henry was no longer running the department—he was now the newspaper's general manager. I would be working for a former retail ad salesman who was now heading the classified department, Darrell Rooney.

My new position meant that I was no longer in the Newspaper Guild Union. I was given a nice salary increase, a membership to the St. Paul Athletic Club, and furnished a company car *(a red 1974 Ford Pinto Hatchback with a lawn mower engine, a four-speed manual transmission and, according to the* National *Safety Council, if rear ended... an exploding gas tank)*. We sold the yellow Mercury, and Susie drove the Malibu while I drove the Pinto with one eye on the rearview mirror.

Jaycees

I got involved with the St. Paul Jaycees and worked my way up in the organization. In 1974 I was elected a director and assigned a new committee called HNR (Human and Natural Resources). It was such a broad title that we could pretty much do anything we wanted. One of our projects was a Haunted House around Halloween. We secured the use of an empty grade school building on the east side of the city, but we couldn't handle a building that big by ourselves. We asked the other Jaycee committees to participate by each taking one classroom to decorate and staff. All of them agreed to do so.

Our room was going to be a spooky, dimly lit cemetery with lots headstones and a few skeletons lying about. We also planned to have zombies (aka the walking dead) jump out at people as they wandered through. (Talk about being ahead of our time!) Red lighting, eerie organ music, and a dry ice fogger added to the overall creepiness. But you couldn't have gravestones on a linoleum floor. The solution? Lots and lots of LEAVES. As it was fall, there were certainly plenty of those. Bonnie, one of our committee members, volunteered to fill bags from her own yard. Ben, another committee member, said he'd haul the leaf filled bags in his pickup truck to the school. Perfect. I loved the cooperation.

The bags arrived, and the leaves scattered around the head-stones and the entire room. It looked absolutely great, but what the hell was that awful smell? Bonnie failed to mention that she had a dog. Watch where you step.

The Good Life

Many of our projects raised money for good causes, but we also did some outreach stuff. One such project was taking a dozen mentally handicapped children on a fishing field trip to Forest Lake—twenty miles north of St. Paul. The group home was to bring them in a large van while the Jaycee volunteers either car pooled or drove their own vehicles. I drove up alone in the Pinto. Several of us arrived early at the lakeside park to load the fishing gear, snacks, and pop onto the two pontoon boats that we had reserved. After the fishing excursion, we cooked hot dogs and hamburgers on the park area grills. The weather had been beautiful and the kids, as well as the adults, all had a good time despite few fish being caught. Best of all, nobody got pierced by a flying fish hook.

It was only around 2:00 p.m. when the kids van pulled out of the parking lot. It was such a gorgeous day that I decided that instead of heading straight home, I'd pay a visit to my friends Ted and Mary Krammer who lived on the north side of Lake Two.

I should explain that Forest Lake is a 2,251 acre lake and it's three lakes in one: The largest is <u>First Lake</u>, and the city's downtown is located on its west bank. That lake narrows on its southeast side, swings a little to the southeast, then opens up into the smallest of the three lakes; <u>Lake Two</u>. At the northeast end of that lake it once again narrows, swings mostly south and opens into <u>Lake Three</u>. All three lakes are easily navigated by boat providing you understand how to avoid the shallow areas.

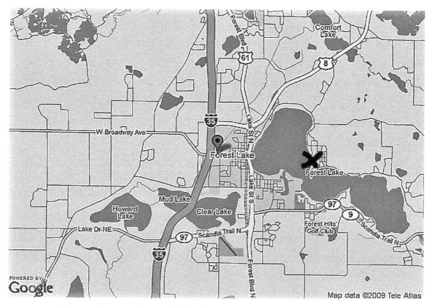

Map of Forest Lake, MN (X is where our house was located

I parked in Krammer's driveway and knocked on the back door. There was no answer, so I walked around to the lakeside and saw Mary sitting down by the beach. She was leaning back in a lawn chair, her eyes were closed, and her face tilted skyward soaking up the warm rays. A bottle of beer adorned her right hand. The lake was busy with various boat types cruising by. The sound of those outboard motors was like music to my ears. I walked silently down and slid into a chair without saying a word. She must have heard something because she opened her eyes, looked over, and laughed. "Golden," she said, "go get yourself a cold beer." Yes, ma'am.

We sat and chatted while enjoying the sun, the serene view and the beer. Ted was out running errands, and I had to get back home, but before leaving I asked, "Hey, Mary, are there any homes or lots for sale around the lake?" She said that there was a lot available just a couple of blocks away on the east side of First Lake. Instead of going up to the main road, I decided to head over the two blocks to Hayward Avenue North to look at that vacant lot. I immediately spotted the "For Sale" sign nailed to a tree, so I parked on the road and walked alongside the densely wooded lot via the next door neighbor's lawn. It was a big lot (80 feet wide by 350 feet deep), but the "beach" was all bulrushes (very tall weeds), lily pads, and mud. On one side there was a relatively new home (I was in their yard) and an old lake cabin stood on the other side. As I walked down by the water, I looked out at the lake and saw where I had started earlier today—Downtown Forest Lake was directly across.

I Needed My Sales Expertise

I told Susie about the fishing expedition and my short visit with Mary. Then I asked, "How would you like to build a house on Forest Lake?"

She said, "You mean a cabin?"

"Nope—a year-round home," I replied.

Then the concerns: (1) it was pretty far out and away from family and friends, (2) the daily commute would be long, (3) Shoreview had great schools—would they be as good in a small town, (4) the cost to build on a lake was high and could we afford to do it. All were reasonable and legitimate questions. She agreed, however, it would be fine to go check it out. The next day the entire family took a drive.

We all stood there looking at the water: Susie; Mike, ten; Bobby, almost eight; Tommy, six; and me. The kids loved the idea of moving to Forest Lake. Maybe a year-round lake house would be a great place to raise the boys. I was surprised to hear Susie say, "Let's do it." We were on our way—let the fun begin!

The owner was asking $17,500 for the property, and my first thought was, *Where on earth am I going to come up that kind of money? Aha—the newspaper credit union.* I didn't think they would be willing to loan me money on a lake lot, but they probably would on a home remodel. So I contacted a Shoreview building contractor and requested a written estimate to convert our current garage into a family room with a fireplace, build a new garage, and construct a huge deck. It all came to $15,000. That worked out fine as we had $3,000 in savings so we could swing the $17,500 lot price. The costs of having house plans drawn, clearing the lot, and the actual construction costs would be another matter. Oh well, one thing at a time. Once I got the fraudulent loan money, I called the lot owner and offered him the asking price, which he accepted. At this point I figured that I was either going to build a house or go to jail.

The St. Paul Jaycees really came in handy. A Jaycee friend, who just happened to be on my old HNR committee, was an attorney. He drew up the lot-purchase contract that protected us by cancelling the agreement in the event that the lot turned out to be unbuildable or, as he had written, "for any other reason." The seller showed up late for the closing, so he felt rushed and only glanced at the contract. Everybody signed, and I handed him a cashier's check. The next day he called me screaming about the "for any other reason" clause. Precisely why you should always read things before signing. But he was stuck, and we could bail for any reason. My attorney's fee was outrageous…a drink at Gallivan's Bar.

Another Jaycee friend was a VP at Minnesota Federal Savings and Loan, and he arranged for us to get a construction loan. I told him that we owned the lot but neglected to mention there was a credit union loan on it. More possible jail time. The remaining mortgage was $26,000 on the Shoreview house, and thankfully it sold quickly for $47,000. Once closed, I could pay off the credit union. So far so good—and no handcuffs yet. *"Bless me, Father, for I have sinned…"*

Yet another Jaycee buddy was an architect. We sat in Gallivan's one evening, and he sketched the floor plan for a two-story home with three bedrooms and two and a half baths on a cocktail napkin. Susie and I both liked the design, so he developed the blueprints. Now all we had to do was hire a general contractor. Money was tight, and I had learned that general contractors charged 10 percent to coordinate everything. I said, "Screw that, I'll do it myself." Now here's a little tip that I learned and will pass on to you in the event you decide to build…for god's sake, **PAY FOR A GENERAL CONTRACTOR.** I still twitch once in a while thinking about our building nightmare.

Hairy Situation

That summer, I took two weeks of vacation in order to figure out how to build a house. I needed to hire a lot of people from a whole host of trades. During that stressful "vacation" period, I decided, just for kicks, to grow a very neatly trimmed beard. I was well aware how unfavorably Bob Momsen, the advertising director, viewed facial hair, so back at work, I tried to lay low. It was midmorning when his secretary called and said, "Mr. Momsen, would like to see you." I knew this was not going to be pleasant. I slowly walked down to his office and stood in his doorway. He glanced up and said, 'Go home and shave that thing off." That was it…he had nothing more to say. I mumbled, "F——— you," under my breath as I turned and walked away.

I'd like to point out that the damn beard was just a whim, and I would have probably gone home and shaved it off if he'd been decent about it. But his autocratic management style pissed me off and consequently brought out my worst. Oh, he wasn't the only one with that style, the ad department management had always been somewhat heavy-handed. I didn't particularly care for that approach, so I promised myself that I would never manage people in that manner. My theory was that if you want buy-in, explain the "why" and not just the "go do." I realized pretty early on that you learned lessons from everybody—the right way to do things as well as the wrong way to do things. The key was to determine which was which.

I admit it, I was annoyed at the "go shave" command. Maybe I still had some of that "I don't back down" kid left in me. I went back to my office and called John Henry, now Bob Momsen's boss. I explained the situation, and after a brief pause, he said, "Well, you know, Tom, even Jesus Christ had a beard. I'll take care of this." I did not shave, and Momsen was livid.

I had won a battle, but had very possibly started a war—with my own boss. A few weeks later, to make peace, I shaved the beard off. I don't think it helped.

Motown

Bob Momsen convinced John that the ad division needed a new management position…a display advertising manager. This individual would be responsible for both retail advertising (stores that sold direct to consumers) as well as national advertising (primarily brand advertising). He was given the green light to interview and then hire. Big surprise—I was not interviewed!

The ultimate hire was a tall, heavyset New Jersey native who was working at the *Detroit Free Press* as a retail advertising sales supervisor (meaning he had a team of outside salespeople reporting to him). His name was Ron Slater (not his real name for reasons which will become evident later), and he looked amazingly like Jonathon Winters.

He seemed to be a nice guy, but it didn't take him long to get into trouble with the sales staffs. I was still in the classified advertising department but attended the weekly retail meetings just to keep up with what was going on. In those meetings Slater had a tendency to talk down to everybody as if he were instructing a kindergarten class. In several he actually used the phrase "puppies and bunnies." The staff thought he was a joke. It became evident to me that he was in way over his head and needed help, and needed it fast. He was desperate to strengthen his management team, which, admittedly, was pretty weak. He told Bob Momsen that he wanted ME. I can't help but wonder about the initial reaction when that request was made. Anyway, in February 1977, I was named retail advertising sales manager. I got a small raise but continued to drive the Pinto. I took over running the weekly sales meetings, and there were no more "puppies and bunnies."

Building the House

Thankfully, my friend Ted's home had been his parents' lake cabin while he was growing up. He had purchased it from them and converted it into a year-round residence. What that meant was that Ted knew EVERYBODY in Forest Lake. "Need trees cut—here's the man to call," "Need the lot graded—talk to this guy," "Need a builder—this fellow might work." And those guys knew other guys, after all, it was a small town. So began my many telephone calls and my frequent trips back and forth to Forest Lake. Trying to coordinate all this while holding down a demanding full time job was most challenging. Then my Graves' disease entered the picture. In case you are not familiar, it is basically an over-performing thyroid. I lost weight, had a heart rate of 110, and frequently had leg cramps (painful charley horses). It was suggested I get treatment at the Mayo Clinic in Rochester, which is only seventy miles south east of St. Paul. So I would drive down to Rochester and then have to drive up to Forest Lake. I nearly lived in my Pinto. Frankly, I was lucky to keep my job. I was more than a little distracted.

Late summer and early fall is a lousy time to start building a new house in Minnesota. By the time we got our permits, cleared the lot, got a well drilled, ran the sewer pipe, and got the foundation built, winter was already on the way. The carpenters worked at a frenzied pace, trying to beat the upcoming freezing temperatures, but failed to do so. Working in November and December was cold and understandably led to more than a few mismeasurements and building mistakes. I had to drive up nearly every day to catch things such as the fireplace foundation being built in the wrong place, a closet walled over, the open staircase had been enclosed, and on and on. I kept calling the HVAC guy to get a furnace-install date, but I got no return calls. Then his wife called to inform me that he had gone bear hunting for two weeks. I do believe this is how you get ulcers.

In late October the new owners of the Shoreview house were ready to move in. We had packed everything up and rented a two-bedroom apartment in Forest Lake. Most of our home's contents were now in storage. At least living in a Forest Lake apartment got the kids enrolled in their new schools and us closer to the construction site.

In an effort to save money, we asked our good friend Bill, a plumber, to do the plumbing at night and on the weekends. We'd help as much as possible and obviously pay him. He had a friend who was an electrician; so he, Bill, and I wired the place. And, to complete the insanity, Susie and I had agreed to stain all the woodwork before it was installed. That meant that each night we'd bundle everybody up and drive over to that freezing house. The carpenters had a small space heater that we cranked up to the max and then attacked the mountain of wood needing stain and varnish: vanities, kitchen cabinets, windows, baseboards, doors, and all of the other assorted trim. First, no general contractor—now this!

Just as we were preparing to move from the apartment into the nearly completed house, my job changed (as I mentioned earlier). I was very skeptical about working for the *Detroit Flash*, but the extra money would certainly come in handy, especially with the new house.

There were still a lot of little things to be completed, but we wanted out of that apartment, so in March, we moved in. The tradesmen would just have to work around us.

Spring came unusually early in 1977, and by April 10, Easter Sunday, it was over eighty degrees. I had desperately wanted to have sod down by Easter, but I couldn't get anybody to deliver that early in the season. The yard remained all dirt as our parents and other invited relatives drove up to see our new home and have Easter dinner.

Summer and winter 22536 Hayward Avenue North, Forest Lake, MN

Willow Point

An old building and several ancient wooden cabins stood on an outcrop of land that separated Lake Two and Lake Three. It was called Willow Point Resort. I think the word "resort" may have been a gross over statement, but they did rent those little cabins in the summer months. The main building contained several businesses: a bar, a grocery store (just the basics), a bait shop (minnows and worms), and a restaurant. Willow was owned by Art & Aggie Cooley, but Aggie pretty much ran the place because Art was busy with his side job as the Forest Lake Township sheriff.

Ted and Mary Krammer ate breakfast at Willow nearly every Saturday morning with their friends Fran and Sue Schlager. Fran was president of a local bank in downtown Forest Lake, and Sue was a school teacher. The Krammers invited us to join them on Saturdays, which we immediately did. It was great fun being with old friends and getting to know some new neighbors. We loved eating breakfast, talking, laughing, and looking out those big windows at the lake.

I had first visited Willow Point some fifteen years earlier when I had driven up to visit Ted in my newly painted '53 Ford. It was 1962, and we were both juniors at Cretin. I was going to spend the night at their lake cabin, which eventually became Ted and Mary's year-round house. I can't recall why we drove over to Willow Point, but suspect it was to buy junk food, pop, or cigarettes. As we walked out of the store, a truck driver making deliveries asked if I'd be interested in selling my car. I wasn't at the time, but I was certainly flattered by the compliment. It sure made all of that hard work on it seem worthwhile.

That next winter we discovered that you could not gauge the crowd inside Willow Point based on the number of cars in the parking lot. In fact, the place could be absolutely jammed, yet the parking lot virtually empty. The reason was snowmobilers. They came roaring in off the lake, and their machines were parked on the lakeside of the building. There could be dozens of them, but none were visible from the road or parking lot.

Walking in you'd be hit with the strong smell of beer and cigarette smoke. It seemed that nearly everybody in Forest Lake smoked.
You didn't need to light up, just breath. You'd also encounter helmets,
snowmobile boots, gloves, and heavy jackets strewn all over the floor.
A lot of people sat at tables with their pants pulled down. Oh, it's not
what you're envisioning, they were actually wearing pants (mostly
jeans) but also one-piece snowmobile suits. To prevent overheating,
they'd either completely remove the suit, or pull it down, and leave it
in a pile at their feet.

Right next to Willow Point is a concrete boat ramp. It would
become my preferred launching place for many years to come.

The Basics

We laid sod on the lakeside of the house and seeded the front
yard. A long driveway had been cut through the woods and covered
with class 5 gravel (crushed limestone and aggregate). That product
compacts easily to create a rock-hard surface. The rest of the natural
forest had been left intact to provide us with privacy from the street.
Additional trees were planted on each side of the driveway right up to
the garage. I wanted to create a "canopy." As the trees matured, I got
my wish. It turned out even better than I had envisioned.

What good is living on a lake if you don't have a boat? But
before actually buying one, I thought it best to create a place to park
one. As pre-built docks were very expensive, I decided to save some
money and build one myself. I went over and looked at Ted and
Mary's dock, then purchased lumber, metal poles and brackets, bolts,
nuts, and nails. I proceeded to build the dock one eight-foot section
at a time. They turned out fine but were extremely heavy. Susie and
the boys helped me haul them down to the beach.

While the house was under construction, we had a number of
truckloads of sand dumped down by the lake to create the appearance of having a sandy beach. I intended to separate the "beach" from
the lawn with railroad ties. It was for looks only as once you stepped
from the sand into the water, you were in mud and muck. Wading

out into it was actually pretty disgusting. Squish, squish, squish as it came up between your toes and swallowed up your feet.

The first dock section went in fine, mainly because most of it was on dry land. I then had to move further and further into the water with each additional section. By the time I got to the last one, I was shoulder deep in the water with goop up well over my ankles and leaches attached to both legs (*C'mon—no big deal, you just peel them off*). I had purchased a couple of old used tires in town and cut a hole in the top of each in order to slide them over two of the dock posts. They would provide the cushioning between the dock and a future boat.

Boating

The ad in the paper read: "*Pontoon and trailer for sale…$200.*" Intriguing…so I drove up to Lindstrom to check them out. As expected, both were REALLY old, but at least the steel floats didn't appear to be rusted through. The seller was kind enough to deliver the pontoon on the trailer and park it in an area that separated our driveway from our neighbor's driveway. The boat came without a motor, but within a week I had paid $50 for an old 15 H.P. outboard motor and a six-gallon gas tank. I installed the motor, then paid a guy with a pick-up truck to launch it next to Willow Point. That heavy old barge was not only slow, it was also truly UGLY. But at least we had something to get us out on the water.

That next spring I was driving home on North Shore Trail when I spotted a silver-blue pontoon boat with a prominent "*For Sale*" sign on it. I stopped, looked it over, and jotted down the phone number. Once again there was no motor; but I liked the fact that it had aluminum, rather than steel, floats. Those made the boat considerably lighter as well as rust free. I called the number, and the asking price was $400. I was currently broke due to so many purchases for the house, so the time had come to have another talk with the credit union. They loved me; after all, I had just recently re-paid them $15,000 for a home improvement loan! In discussing the $400 loan, it occurred to me that putting that old fifteen-horse motor on that "new" boat just wouldn't be right. I ended up borrowing enough to buy the pontoon boat AND a new 25 H. P. Johnson outboard motor.

Me, Tom, Jr., with Mike in the water, 1978

Shortly after placing an ad in the local Forest Lake weekly, I sold the "old" boat with the steel floats, the 15 H. P. motor, and the trailer for $250. Hurray—I broke even.

Before launching the "new" boat, I re-painted the silver blue front panels a bright sunshine yellow. You'd be able to see us coming from a long ways off! After installing the new 25 H. P. motor, it was all set to go. It certainly looked better parked at our dock than that old one.

I decided to jazz up the pontoon a little more by adding some running lights so we could take it out at night. Ted's beach had a beautiful sand bottom, so I asked if I might do the under boat wiring next to his dock. He said, "Yah, shure, you betcha." You probably saw *Fargo* and just assume that all Minnesotans talk that way. We do.

It was midsummer and hot, so the lake water was warm. I was under the boat running wire, wearing only swim trunks. I knelt on the firm sandy lake bottom, and the water came up to my shoulders. Because the pontoon floats made the boat ride high in the water, I had plenty of head room to work. Ted sat on the dock drinking a beer, and we talked back and forth while I worked. All of a sudden a small fish, possibly a baby Northern Pike about four inches long, began darting at my chest. I kept brushing it away, but it kept coming back. I told Ted, and he just laughed. After all, this was Minnesota—not exactly piranha country. Fish here don't attack…or so I thought.

While my arms were up under the pontoon attaching the wires, the damn thing darted in and bit me—right in the nipple. I came up out of the water fast, and there was a stream of blood running down my chest. Ted had just taken a swig of beer, and when he saw me, that beer spewed out his nose and his mouth like a fountain. Yeah, absolutely hilarious, Ted. My nipple hurt.

Another Boat

Our national advertising rep firm, Knight-Ridder Newspaper Sales, had offices in various cities around the country. Their job was to convince national advertisers to run newspaper advertising in our companies various markets. One such office was in downtown Minneapolis, and they made sales calls on companies such as 3M, Hormel, Land O' Lakes, Pillsbury, and General Mills on our behalf, as well as all the other Knight-Ridder newspapers.

The Minneapolis office manager, Don Hansen, was in my office one day; and I told him about our new home on Forest Lake. He broke into a big grin and said, "Want to buy a speed boat?" He explained that it was a 1976 blue-and-white fourteen-and-a-half-foot Glastron tri-hull with a 50 H.P outboard engine. He said that he had bought it new and it was still "mint" because he had only used it a few times. It was parked on a trailer under a tarp in his garage. His asking price of $1,500 for the whole package seemed like a good deal. I agreed to drive over to his house in Minneapolis over the weekend. He hadn't exaggerated; it looked as if it had just come off the show floor. The outboard motor ran on a mix of regular unleaded gas with one small can of oil added to each six-gallon tank (also included). He had the case of twenty-four oil cans that originally came with the boat, and only two cans were missing.

It was back to the credit union!

Now there was a boat parked on each side of my dock: a screamin' yellow pontoon (with running lights) and a brand-new-looking speed boat. I felt like "King of the Hill" just looking out at them.

The Open Waters

We all loved the lake, and the boating was so much fun. I was able to pull the kids up one at a time on water skis with the runabout. The 50 H.P. motor, however, didn't have enough power to "pop" them right up—so they got dragged a little first. The pontoon boat was for slow-paced relaxation. Sometimes we'd put a small grill on the front deck and cook chicken, burgers, or hot dogs while drifting around in the middle of the lake. Lake living was indeed fantastic.

As the leaves began to turn and the temperatures cool, I had to start thinking about pulling both boats out of the water and removing the dock for winter. It was always sad when the boating season ended because it meant six to seven months before we'd launch again.

Lots of Ice

The lake froze, and the snow flew. Our boys constructed hockey nets out of old lumber and chicken wire fencing…pretty crude and heavy, but they'd work just fine. They shoveled off a rink in front of the house and then flooded it with our garden hose in order to make the surface smooth (we had no Zamboni). The nets were moved into position, and they were set to play hockey—and they did for hours on end.

All winter long they shoveled snow off that rink. When we got hit by heavy snowfalls or there were big snowdrifts, one of the neighborhood dads would come over with a pick-up and plow it. We noticed that in Forest Lake, nearly every pick-up truck had a plow on the front all winter long.

The spotlights on the front of the house did a very poor job of lighting the rink for night play. The boys had a fix: (1) Chop holes in the ice about eight feet behind the nets at each end of the rink until water was hit, (2) drop in tall poles, (3) push the poles into the muddy lake bottom for stability,(4) pack snow and ice chunks around the poles to keep them straight. Ice would re-form overnight making the poles solid, sturdy, and ready for (5) the installation of flood lights. Long extension cords could be run from the rink lights to the electrical outlet on the deck. A well thought-out plan, so I bought the poles, lights, and extension cords and they did the rest. It was so cool to look out the window and see all three of our boys, and their friends, skating around on a lighted hockey rink.

We Confiscate the Rink

I wanted to have a big Christmas party at our house for all the ad division managers and their spouses. Susie knew most of them from various get-togethers so she agreed. Plans were made, and the invitations, which included the wording, "Bring warm clothes and two brooms," were sent out. We were a little afraid that the twenty-five-mile trek to our house might discourage some from attending, but EVERYBODY said yes—including my boss, Ron Slater. I think all were intrigued by the cryptic instructions in the invitation. I steadfastly refused to discuss that subject when asked at work.

The party would be nothing fancy: a mix-your-own bar setup, chips and dip, nuts, a veggie tray, some candy and Christmas cookies, and, later in the evening, hot sloppy Joe's.

As people arrived, armed with their brooms, we explained that we were all going out on the lake to play broom ball. It was like hockey, but brooms took the place of hockey sticks, and a soccer ball substituted for the puck. The rink was lit, the nets were in place, and we were set to go except for one problem…the temperature was ten below zero.

Before venturing out, people wanted to get a little antifreeze into their systems. After a couple of pops, everybody got bundled up and headed outside. I asked for goalie volunteers, chose two, and then the teams were determined (no spouses could be on the same team). Then things got rough in a hurry. Ad people tend to be very competitive by nature; and there was a lot more pushing, shoving, and *CHECKING* than we had ever anticipated. They were all laughing, but at the same time, taking the game pretty seriously.

The ball got batted around until someone smacked it hard past the goalie and into the net. "***GOAL***," shouted that team in unison with their arms raised in the air. "***BOO—LUCKY SHOT***," some on the opposing team yelled. We were out there running around on the ice, trying to stay warm for about fifteen minutes, when something unexpected happened...the ball got whacked and broke into five pieces. The below zero temps had frozen it solid, and it got brittle. Who knew? The game was over, so the bar re-opened. Everyone crowded around the fireplace to thaw out.

The party was a "smashing" success, and we vowed to do it again the next year.

Discovery

When the snow and the ice began to melt in the spring, it was time to bring in the hockey nets and take down the spotlights. The poles were frozen solid into the ice and chipping them out would be a tough job. We decided to let nature take care of it—when the ice melted, the poles would fall and float to shore (at least that was our hope).

I leaned a ladder against the poles and removed the lights, then began to reel in the extension cords. That was when I made a most shocking discovery—there were six-inch stretches of extension cord with absolutely no covering left on them at all. Just bare copper wire. The plastic covering had apparently frozen, gotten brittle (like the soccer ball), and broken off as the boys walked over the cords with their skate blades. I'm still amazed that didn't pop a circuit breaker—or zap one of the kids.

Motown Part Two

Ron Slater relied heavily on his secretary to keep track of everything for him. That being the case, he developed a rather odd habit—each Friday afternoon, before leaving for the weekend, he would clear off his entire desk and credenza. By "clear off," I mean *throw everything away*. It all went into his waste basket. I guess he just wanted a fresh start each Monday. One of the things that he inadvertently discarded was a memo from his boss, Bob Momsen, requesting a detailed report on some damn thing. Like many companies, we did reports on reports. There was far too much cover-your-ass paperwork.

The day after the report had been due, Momsen walked into Slater's office and asked where it was. Much to my dismay, and apparently in a moment of panic, Slater responded, "I asked Tom Golden to do that report. Let me see if he's finished with it." I didn't know it yet, but I had just been thrown under the bus. Then he did the unthinkable, he called in his secretary, dictated a memo addressed to me requesting the report, backdated the memo by a week, tore up the original copy and kept only the carbon copy (as if the original had been sent to me the prior week). He then had his secretary make a copy of that memo and deliver it to Momsen's in-box with the notation "FYI" (for your information). Slater then walked into my office with the memo carbon copy in hand and asked "Where's this report?" HUH? I had obviously never seen that memo before. I was pretty darn efficient and wondered how on earth I could have missed it. It seemed rather odd…and it sure made me look bad.

Over the years, I made it a practice to be nice to everybody regardless of their department, their position, or their responsibilities at the paper. My theory had always been, "Be nice to everybody on the way up, because when you end up in hot water, which eventually you will, these are the folks who can either save you or sink you." Besides, everybody deserves respect (providing they don't forfeit it).

For the ad division secretaries, none of whom worked directly for me, I always had a birthday card for each; a small box of candy on Valentine's Day; and a little gift, like a tree ornament, at Christmas. Think that doesn't mean a lot? They were underpaid and felt underappreciated, so a little bit of recognition went a long way.

Late that afternoon, with Momsen at a meeting outside of the building, Slater decided to leave early. He was gone, but his secretary remained. I walked over to her desk holding the memo in my hand, bent down low, and quietly asked, "Chris, when did you type this memo?" She looked at me and then hung her head and stared at the top of her desk. Her shoulders began to shake as she started crying. After a few seconds of painful silence, she whispered, "This afternoon." As I walked back to my office I mumbled, "Why, that son-of-a-bitch."

The next morning I walked into Momsen's office and asked that we talk. He could see that I was visibly upset but said that he had an executive meeting to attend upstairs. Then he unexpectedly asked, "Are you free for lunch?" He NEVER invited me to lunch, so he must have sensed that something ugly was brewing. I agreed and returned to my office.

At noon we walked together up to the Minnesota Club (your typical paneled wall, crystal chandelier, exclusive private club). This is where all of the "big kids" ate. We were seated in the dining room, and Bob started with small talk—but NOT ME. I pulled out the memo and proceeded to tell him what had transpired. I then looked him straight in the eye and said, "Either he goes or I go." He seemed shocked at the chain of events that I had outlined and promised to immediately look into it. I'm sure he knew that doing little or nothing would most likely result in me calling John Henry, who was now the publisher. That would certainly not reflect well on him. I'm sure he also realized that if my accusation was true, he really had no choice but to terminate Slater.

There must have been meetings that very afternoon because early the next morning a memo was issued indicating that Ron Slater had a family emergency back in New Jersey. It went on to say he could be gone an extended period of time. I was told in private that he would never be returning.

One month later, a memo was issued announcing that Mr. Slater had decided to accept a position close to his home in New Jersey. He would not be returning. Darrell Rooney, the classified advertising manager, would replace him as display advertising manager. I was then promoted to classified advertising manager. I realized that I now occupied the same position that John Henry had held some thirteen years earlier when I interviewed. That was a true source of pride.

One, Two, Three—Shift

Two years later (1981), I had just returned from the annual classified ad manager's conference in Chicago. While there, I was elected to the association's board of directors. I was pretty excited about that honor and the fact that I was getting some recognition within the industry.

It was my first day back when I got a call from Bob Momsen's secretary, Betty, saying that he wanted to see me. I walked into his office, and he asked me to sit down. He then pushed the button under his desk that closed his office door. Seriously, he really had a door closing button. "Tom, I've decided to make some changes." Oh no, a closed door combined with an opening statement like that usually didn't end with good news. "I'm going to put Darrell back in Classified, and I want you to take over as display advertising manager." I was getting bounced back and forth between classified and display like a ping-pong ball. He outlined my new package: I would now be responsible for two-thirds of the total ad division revenues, be given a salary increase with additional bonus potential, and assigned a new a 1981 Ford Fairlane company car. Bye, bye, Classified!

My Three Sons

Growing up on the lake had its perks. Besides the year-round lake activities, there was also golf. We had joined Forest Hills Country Club, which was located about a mile south of Lake Two. The three boys would load their bicycles and their clubs onto the pontoon boat, then drive over and park it on the Lake Two shoreline. They'd sling the golf bags over their shoulders and ride over to the clubhouse. Like most private golf clubs, Forest Hills accepted no cash—everything had to be charged to the membership number and purchases were billed once a month. It was not a fancy golf club, but rather a small town or "working man's" club back then. No big pretentious club house, just a white-sided building that held a bar/restaurant, pro shop, and locker rooms. But the dining room did have large windows overlooking the eighteenth green. I hated putting there because I knew that people were watching...and laughing. The membership fee to join was $500 (refundable when you left the club) and there was a $75 monthly minimum food and beverage charge. Between the hot dogs, burgers, fries, pop, and candy that the kids regularly scarfed down, meeting our monthly minimum was never a problem. Exceeding it by a wide margin was the problem.

Between the boating, water skiing, swimming, fishing, and golf, they had plenty of summer activities. All three boys had deep tans during the summer months as they were outside most of the time. If they came in on a beautiful day to watch TV, Susie would throw them back out. There would be no couch potato behavior in our family (other than mine).

Those tans faded, however, once winter arrived. The cold could sometimes be just brutal. As our home was on the east side of First Lake, we were hit with the howling wind that came across it from the northwest. Over the years, we had encountered wind chill temperatures as low as -70 *(yes, seventy below zero)*. But, thankfully, it wasn't always that frigid. There were many days when temperatures zoomed into the twenties. On those warm days you'd occasionally see guys at the mall wearing shorts.

Besides the hockey rink, I thought a couple of snowmobiles might be fun. Our debt load was already sufficiently high, and I had no desire to visit my friends at the credit union again, so I bought two old used machines. One cost $150 and the other piece of junk was $50. Both had pull start engines, and both were stubborn starters.

Because of the frigid weather, we also had to purchase snowmobile suits, boots, gloves, and helmets. The cost of all that gear for the entire family far exceeded the cost of the two machines. Riding was great fun and on occasion, Susie and I joined the snowmobile crowd at Willow Point for a "warm-up." I suspect that many looked out and chuckled as we pulled up on our crappy old sleds.

The boys failed to tell us that simply riding a snowmobile was not enough…they had to "jump" them. Jumping required building a ramp and then hitting it at top speed. The result was going airborne. Thankfully, Susie and I were blissfully unaware of those activities.

I was actually the one who broke a ski while snowmobiling with Ted alongside Hwy. 97 in Scandia. I hit a culvert and snapped it right in half. I had to ride all the way back home standing and leaning to one side trying to keep the broken ski off the ground. Ted laughed as he rode alongside of me on his new Arctic Cat.

Vacation

Sure, we lived on a lake, but for some reason felt the need to "vacation" on some other lake.

It was the summer of 1981, and we loaded up the car for a trip north to Itasca State Park to stay in a lake cabin. Itasca is a huge park with a big lake, a log lodge, and rentable camp sites and log cabins. Because the cabins are so popular, you have to reserve them well in advance. The parks real claim to fame is that it contains the headwaters of the mighty Mississippi River. You can literally walk across the river on the rocks and boulders, much like crossing a small stream.

The cabin we reserved consisted of two bedrooms, a living room/kitchen, a bathroom, and a large-screened front porch. It was close to the lake and surrounded by tall trees. Numerous identical cabins were scattered throughout the area, and all were connected by a wide gravel walkway. Following that path from our cabin's front door, we passed five or six other cabins on our way to and from the lodge.

Upon checking in we were told, "Do not feed the raccoons." We had no intention of feeding any raccoons, squirrels, black bears, or any other wild animals. Why on earth would they tell us that? After we settled in, we drove over to Douglas Lodge for dinner. It was still light out when we returned to our cabin, so we decided to sit at the card table on the front porch and play UNO. After all, we were roughing it—NO TV!

The game went on as the sun set, so I turned on the ceiling light. Shortly after doing so, there was a knock at the door. Who could that be? I went to the door, looked out, but there was nobody there. I went back and sat down. Once again there was a knock-knock. What on earth? I went back to the screen door, looked out, nobody there. This time I flipped on the outside spot lights, and the mystery was solved. There at the bottom of the steps stood a raccoon. It was sitting up on its hind legs and begging like a dog. I called everybody over to witness this crazy animal act. It stood there for maybe a minute, and when we didn't offer any food, it turned around and walked down the path to the next cabin. We all watched as it climbed the steps, knocked on the door with a front paw, then walked back down the steps, and sat up and begged. We guessed that visiting each cabin was probably a nightly ritual. Now we understood that warning at the lodge: "Don't feed the raccoons."

The next day we rented a fishing boat but had no luck catching anything. We then walked some of the wooded trails, rode around the park on rented bikes, and finally ended up at the headwaters. We all had to walk across the Mississippi river just to say that we had.

That night we drove twenty miles to the town of Park Rapids to see the new movie *Raiders of the Lost Ark*. The boys and I absolutely loved it... Susie, not so much.

We all got bored "roughing it," so we cut the vacation short and drove back to our own lake.

Meow

Susie was allergic to most animals, so that ruled out having a dog or cat (or so we thought). One evening, we sat down for dinner at the kitchen table, which was positioned directly in front of the sliding glass door leading out to the deck. It was warm, and the house not air conditioned; so all the windows, including the sliding glass door, were open. Obviously, each had a screen to keep out all the flying insects. *(Because of all of the water, Minnesota has a rather large mosquito population.)*

Susie was bringing food to the table when she exclaimed, "Look, a little kitten is hanging on the screen door." Sure enough, there it was, but where on earth had it come from? Nobody knew. It must be a stray. Then the kids begging started:

"Can we keep it?"

"NO," Susie said.

"But, Mom..."

"NO."

"Please, Mom…"

And the whining and the pleading continued throughout dinner. The kitten had jumped down and now stood on the deck, staring in at us. She was so little and so darn cute. Finally, Susie asked a question that I'm sure she instantly regretted: "Who will feed and take care of it?" I have no idea what kind of answer she had expected, but what came back was a resounding, "WE WILL, MOM." Oh yeah, you can take that to the bank. And so, *Mindy* became a part of our family, and Susie sneezed a lot. Guess who ended up taking care of that kitty? You didn't actually speculate "the kids," did you?

If you suspected that the kitty on the screen door was a "con job," you were right. It was sometime later that we learned the "stray kitten" was actually one from a litter at a friend's house. The boys had brought it home and then hatched a plan: two of them would come inside and distract us while the third would hang the little cutie on the screen door. Then one of the "inside gang" would stand in front of the screen to block the view and prevent us from seeing it. The outside man then ran around the house and came in through the side door. Everybody was present and accounted for, so we all sat down. All of a sudden the kitten was "discovered." Good plan, perfect execution, and ultimate success. How could Susie and I have been so naïve?

Fast forward a year or so and once again we were all gathered around the kitchen table for dinner. Mindy had been under the table, and as usual, rubbing up against everybody's legs. After dinner she walked over towards the kitchen where she stopped and froze. I looked over at her and said, "Why don't you do something useful like catch a mouse?" The word "mouse" had barely crossed my lips when she pounced on a little mouse that emerged from under the refrigerator. We all laughed as the timing was so uncanny.

Because we had dense woods in back and on one side of the house, field mice were pretty common. It was, however, very uncommon for one to actually make its way into the house. Maybe having a cat around was a good idea.

Things Change

As the boys got a little older, Susie had quit smoking and, for the most part, drinking as well. Instead of watching TV with me at night, she sat and read the Bible and various other books…all were of a religious nature. She had joined a small non-denominational church and attended their Sunday service. I did not attend with her. They all took the Bible pretty literally, and it was too intense for me.

Okay, let me be clear, even though I had twelve years of Catholic education, I am not an overly religious person… BUT neither am I anti-religion. I do not have anything against the various forms of Christianity, Buddhism, Islam, Judaism, Hinduism, or most any other religion. Here's the bottom line as far as I'm concerned… ONE GOD…many ways to worship.

It seems to me, however, that the more fanatical and intractable a person's religious beliefs, the more self-righteous, judgmental, and intolerant they may become of others actions, beliefs, and lifestyles. People who do not believe as they do can become fair game to criticize or even condemn. I just can't go along with that.

Religion is such a personal thing, and it is certainly not my intention to be critical of evangelicals and their deep-rooted beliefs. I'm only trying to point out that our marriage began to crumble because Susie and I viewed so many things from a different perspective. And let's face it, arguing about that does no good.

So I humbly request that you not judge me. Please leave that to God. Surely you know that He is infinitely more qualified! *(I know, don't call me Shirley.)*
Moving on.

Expansion

In the summer of 1983, we decided to expand our living space by adding a new room to the house. I was the designer and the general contractor. *(Wouldn't you think I'd learn?)* The eighteen-by-twenty-six-foot room would have a cathedral ceiling and serve two purposes: one half would contain a pool table and the other half would be a cozy family room with a wood-burning, old-Chicago brick fireplace. The addition would be one step down from the rest of the house and accessed from the living room through French doors. There would be lots of windows, including a large picture window, to flood the room with natural light.

As construction progressed, I purchased a new pool table, pool table light, six-cue wall rack, six cues, a bridge stick, triangle, balls, felt brush, chalk, and a table cover from Peter's Billiards in Minneapolis. When the room was finally finished, the furnishings for the pool table side were delivered and setup. We then moved our nearly new Flexsteel sofa and love seat from the living room into the family room. The matching winged-back colonial pieces were oversized and very comfortable. We were told that the blue, brown, and beige heavy-duty country plaid fabric would wear forever. It did. We then purchased new, more formal furniture for the living room.

The builders had done a marvelous job of insulating…the room was "tight." In fact, we learned the hard way, exactly how tight. I put kindling on the fireplace grate, then a couple of softwood birch logs on top. Once the fire got going, I would add nothing but oak logs from that point on. Oak is a hardwood that burns much hotter than soft woods. It creates less creosote that can build up and line the chimney. I opened the damper and then lit some newspaper and pushed it under the grate. The burning paper started the kindling on fire, and that is when smoke began billowing out filling the entire room.

I was panicky—what do I do? I knew the damper was open— why wasn't it drawing? I jumped up and quickly closed the French doors that led into the living room to prevent the entire house from filling with smoke. My eyes watered, and my throat burned as I ran around cranking open all the windows. Smoke then poured outside. Thankfully, the neighbors didn't call the fire department. Well, it was a volunteer fire department and they wouldn't have arrived for quite a while anyway. Then, like a miracle, the smoke stopped pouring into the room and began going up the chimney. I turned on the ceiling fan and left all the windows open until the air finally cleared. After that the sofa and love seat emitted a slight smoky odor. I thought it added to the room's charm and ambience… Susie not so much.

We learned that when it was really cold outside, we had to "warm the chimney." That entailed allowing some fresh air to enter the room by either cracking open the door that led outside or cranking open a window. We'd then warm the flue by lighting some newspaper and holding it up near the open damper. Sometimes there would initially be a down draft that would send a little smoke into the room, but once it began to draw, we were fine. We loved the cracking of a real wood fire but always had to keep the fireplace screen in position as those "snaps and pops" could shoot burning embers right out into the room. And I felt VERY manly splitting logs in the driveway with my axe.

When guests came over on cold winter evenings, a favorite place for them to sit was on the raised hearth and soak up the heat from the fire. They'd rave about how warm, cozy, and inviting our new room was. The guys in particular loved the pool table. We played many a game while the wives sat and talked by the fire. It quickly became our favorite room in the whole house.

As Susie got more and more involved in religion and her church, I spent a lot more time out on the lake. I especially loved Sunday mornings just drifting around on the pontoon. It was so quiet and peaceful with few other boats around except a few fishermen. They tended to stay close to shore in shallower water near the weed beds.

Family photo taken around 1985: I shaved off my moustache and two of the boys grew them! Bob is on the left, then Susie, Mike in back and Tom, Jr.

Rock and Roll

Tommy, our youngest, wanted to play in the junior high marching band and had chosen the trumpet as his instrument. Instead of renting one, we went ahead and purchased one for him. Then, I guess because that instrument was paid for and too easy to carry around, he switched to the TUBA. I said, "We are not buying one of those things." We did rent one, though. Thankfully, we found a trumpet buyer.

Meanwhile, Mike and Bob started a rock band called *ASYLUM*. They frequently practiced in our garage with Mike playing the drums and Bob on the bass guitar. Assorted friends added additional amplified guitars and vocals. Poor Tommy and his tuba were taboo. *That line was kinda fun to write.*

The music boomed out of our garage and could be heard for blocks around. Thankfully, the neighbors were kind enough not to complain (or call the police). As far as teenage garage bands went, they were actually pretty good but their choice of songs left something to be desired. They played such popular tunes as "Cocaine" by Eric Clapton and other delightful songs by Black Sabbath. What parent doesn't want those lyrics blasting out of their garage? Susie and I were a little aghast at some of the words.

The "boys" decided that it would be great fun to play in our garage on Halloween night. As children, some with their parents, walked down our long driveway with trick-or-treat bags, the garage door opened and the band belted out... *"If you want to go out, you've got to take her out—COCAINE."* Ah, the very words that Mom and Dad whisper to their little ones at bedtime. Instead of attracting hordes of screaming female groupies, the loud music scared most everyone off. We gave out virtually no candy that year, so we all got a little extra sugar in our diets.

The band eventually "dis-banded," and Tommy's tuba practicing gave way to cross-country running and racquetball. It was certainly much quieter around the house...and the neighbor's started talking to us again!

Smoking and Running (Not at the Same Time)

Four of us at the newspaper had decided that we'd all quit smoking. Each day we'd put a dollar into a coffee can, meaning that we hadn't smoked (it was the honor system). The idea was that if you re-started, you would forfeit the money that you had put into the can. The money would go to the "last man standing" or, on the first anniversary of the bet, be divided equally amongst the survivors. The can filled up, so we opened a credit union savings account. Two of the four eventually split the dough on the one-year anniversary of the bet. I had hung in there and quit my pack-a-day habit cold turkey. But I had ongoing and very realistic dreams of smoking. Sometimes I'd wake up and wonder if I had actually given in to temptation.

The other successful quitter had taken up running, and he had lost considerable weight in doing so. I thought I'd give running a try as well. I was only thirty-eight but overweight and out of shape. I purchased some New Balance 990 running shoes and began trudging along for a few blocks early each morning. I had to stop frequently to catch my breath. Soon my legs ached, and I developed chin splints because I wasn't stretching enough before my outdoor "runs." But I'm pretty competitive; so I stretched more, started keeping a daily diary, and just ran through the pain. I felt compelled to increase either my distance or my speed each day. Eventually I was intent on doing BOTH.

The few blocks turned into a mile, then two, then three, then four, then five, and some days six. My ten-minute miles became nine, then eight, then seven and a half. My weight dropped dramatically. I fell from 195 to 154. As a guy six feet tall, I looked pretty thin at that weight. People honestly thought that I was ill because I had lost the weight so quickly. I looked gaunt, and my clothes just hung on me. I had to replace my entire wardrobe starting with my "work clothes." New suits, sport coats, shirts, and belts were not inexpensive.

*A very slender version of me running a 10K race in
1986. The beard was grey even back then*

I ran five or six miles each weekday morning and increased that
to eight miles on Saturday. I took Sunday off to give my body a
much-needed rest. I continued this regimen for sixteen years regardless of weather conditions or travel schedules. I was like the post
office—neither rain, nor sleet, nor heat, nor gloom of night kept
me from my appointed rounds. When traveling, I absolutely loved
running around the cities that I visited. But the constant pounding
on the concrete and the asphalt eventually caught up with my knees.
I stopped running, but my knees were not the reason.

Independence

Mike, our oldest, decided that after his high school graduation
he would move out of the house. A couple of his buddies were renting a small home in Scandia (still in the Forest Lake area) and invited
him to join them.

As a parent, it is a sad day when a child leaves the nest: many go off to college, others enlist in the military, some find a job and want a place of their own…still others, like Susie and I, get married at a tender age. No matter what the reason, when they go off and into their new adventure, you are left with a gaping hole in your life. Susie and I were both absolutely brokenhearted. I recall walking into Mike and Bob's room after he had left and bursting into tears. Time was marching on, and we didn't want it to. Our little boy, the one who sat out on the roof, who painted the neighbor's sidewalk, who hung a kitten on the screen door, who played drums in a rock and roll garage band was gone. Life would go on, but it would never be quite the same.

Bob, on the other hand, did not seem overly saddened by his big brothers departure. He had been sharing a bedroom with Mike for his entire life. Now he finally had a room of his own. He quickly redecorated by replacing the two beds with a large water bed (all the rage back then). My concern was whether the floor joists could handle that weight load. They did.

For Bob's sixteenth birthday we gave him a new, and might I add expensive, Ibanez Iceman bass guitar. He practiced in his room frequently and got very good. He recently told me that he still plays it.

Big Promotion

In December 1984, just before our annual Christmas/Broomball party, I was named advertising director. I was now in charge of the entire ad division. It was a very prestigious and high-profile job to hold in St. Paul, Minnesota, as most households still subscribed to the daily newspaper. Bob Momsen was now vice president of marketing and was moved out of advertising and up to the executive offices. I was given a raise, a new office, membership to the Minnesota Club, and the promise of a nicer company car. About a year later I was assigned a new a Mercury Sable that looked like a jelly bean. Susie's sisters began calling us The Jetsons because of that "futuristic" automobile. They also said we were "jet-setters" because of our travels. We were hardly that. As for Susie's dad, we continued to get along fine.

Susie 2.0

The Bible and the other religious books had become constant reading. To those were added religious records, tapes, magazines, brochures, pamphlets, and extended telephone conversations. Her friends tended to be people with similar religious beliefs…some I met, others I never did. I'm sure this was totally unintended, but I felt that she was slipping away from me. I suspected that she had been unhappy with me, or our marriage, or possibly life in general. Now she had found something that provided her with peace, comfort, and joy. She was happy—I was not.

Her once somewhat liberal views turned decidedly more conservative. Then they turned ultraconservative. All things were now being "filtered" through her new, and pretty intense, belief system. Things that had once been "gray" were now either "black or white." Our interests had become decidedly different—sometimes even at odds. We were more guarded in the things that we discussed or said to each other. While I honestly believe that we still loved each other, I felt that her new convictions and attitudes were causing us to drift further and further apart.

At one point I came right out and asked her, "Am I the same person that you married?" She thought for a moment and replied, "Yes, you are." I then said, "Well, you are not the same person that I married." She smiled and said, "I know." She so desperately wanted to convert me. I so desperately wanted my old Susie back. Neither of us ended up getting what we wanted.

New Toys

In 1987, my title was changed to "Vice President, Advertising Director." It was the same job, just more money and a fancier title… and a nicer company car.

It was time to get rid of the "yellow beast" and buy a new pontoon boat. I purchased a sixteen-foot Sun Tracker Bass Buggy with a 50 H. P. Johnson outboard motor. It had everything: tilt and trim on the motor, twin six-gallon gas tanks, Bimini top, carpeted deck, leather upholstered seating, a big swivel captain's chair behind a huge console with the steering wheel, engine controls, AM/FM/cassette tape stereo system, depth gauge, aerated live well, and built-in cooler. There was storage for life jackets under the seats, and to protect everything from the elements, there was a canvas tie-down tarp. It was DELUXE all the way.

I then decided that I couldn't park that gorgeous new boat next to that crappy, old wooden dock with the tires hanging off the posts. I mean, how crass would that be? So my master plan began on the shoreline where I built a stone patio with a lamppost surrounded by shrubs and flower pots. A garden bench was added to complete the look I was after. Then came the most exciting part of the project, I connected a brand-new carpeted aluminum dock to it. From the dock I hung real boat bumpers. The final touch was a tall pole with a flag design windsock. It looked spectacular.

Wiring Wizard

There's a little back story regarding that lamppost. When we built the house in 1976, I had always envisioned a lamppost out by the dock, so we wired accordingly. The lamppost wire ran from the breaker box into a multi-switch box located next to the sliding glass door in the kitchen. I insisted, however, that the line be capped in the box just from a safety standpoint. From the wall switch box, the wire ran down the inside the exterior wall, into the crawl space, then out and under the deck. It sat there coiled up, just waiting for the day that it would be connected to a new lamppost.

Around the deck, which ran the full width of the house on the lakeside, I created a landscape area and planted various shrubs. That planting area was framed with old railroad ties.

Since building the house, we had done a complete kitchen renovation that included replacing a cheap six-foot sliding glass door, with a not-so-cheap nine-foot Pella sliding glass door. In order to install the wider door, the wall switches had to be moved over. Unbeknownst to me, the electrician found that unconnected capped wire in the box and connected it to a switch. So the NOT LIVE wire under the deck became a LIVE WIRE when the switch was turned on. That would have been good to know.

One Saturday morning, I decided to run the wire from my new lamppost by the beach up to the house. It was a good time to do it because the rain had made the ground nice and soft. It would be easy to dig a trench under the grass to bury the wire. Because it was quite warm despite a light drizzle, I wore only shorts and a tee-shirt.

This job would require only a few tools: something to cut the wire (a pair of tin snips would work), something to bare the wire ends (a razor blade should be just fine), a couple of twist cap connectors, and maybe a little electrical tape. Now my tin snips were very old and all metal. They did not have any rubber or plastic on the grips. Well, they were tin snips—not wire cutters. I did the wiring on the lamppost first, then ran the wire underground up to the deck. At that point I'd simply connect the wire to the one that had been waiting patiently for the past decade. I reached under the deck and pulled out the coiled wire.

Meanwhile, inside the house, the lamppost wall switch was in the ON position. I don't know why, but I never bothered to check because I was still under the impression that it wasn't connected anyway.

Kneeling on the wet railroad tie, my bare feet resting in the wet grass and my hands wet from the rain, I carefully measured how much wire had to be cut off. I gripped the metal tin snips in my right hand and cut into the wire. Instantaneously, there was a crisp electrical *ZZZZZAAP* sound and a simultaneous flash of blue shot from the cut wire. *What the hell?* How could a not live wire nearly kill me? Then, looking at the sliding glass door, it finally dawned on me that the switches had been moved when we remodeled. DUH!

The new pontoon, the new dock and the lamp post that almost killed me

Here's the strange thing, I didn't even get a shock. I felt nothing at all—not even a tingle. That just seems to defy logic. I got up and went inside to check the breaker box, and sure enough, the circuit breaker had popped. That breaker saved my life. I went back out, connected the wires, flipped the breaker back on, and bingo, the lamppost was lit.

If it weren't for that circuit breaker, I'm sure that my headstone would have probably read:

> **Thomas R. Golden**
> **May 24, 1945–July 18, 1987**
> **Dumbass was fried when he failed to turn off a light switch. He tried wiring with live wires. It's really hard to feel sorry for him.**

Chapter 6

Chapter 6

Recruited

In the early spring of 1991, I received a call from Brian Ray, a newspaper headhunter in Atlanta. He asked if I might be interested in moving South: "How far south?" I asked, answering a question with a question. He said that he was not at liberty to say at the moment. "Look," I said, "I'm forty-six years old, and I've never lived anywhere but the Twin Cities in my whole life. My concern in asking how far south is my fear of not fitting into a totally different culture and, for that matter, being accepted." I had heard that "Yankees" weren't universally beloved in the southern states. His reply was, "Oh, I totally understand. Would you be willing to fly into the Atlanta airport? I could have a car bring you over to the Hilton Hotel where we could talk." Well, it's always flattering to be wanted, so I agreed to fly down.

Brian was waiting for me in a small conference room at the airport Hilton. The interview questions and our conversation all seemed pleasant enough, and we seemed to hit it off. While still being elusive regarding the actual location of the opportunity, he did promise to get back to me soon. I flew back to St. Paul not knowing any more than when I had flown in.

A couple of days later my office phone rang and it was Brian wondering if I might like to fly to Birmingham, Alabama, for a visit with the publisher and the general manager of *The Birmingham News*. The first word out of my mouth was about two octaves higher than normal, "BIRMINGHAM? I thought we discussed my hesitation and fear of moving to the DEEP South." The only thing that I knew about Birmingham was that the state license plate slogan was "*The*

Heart of Dixie," and I recalled several news reports that I had seen on TV back in the sixties. It was all pretty memorable stuff: civil rights marches, demonstrations, baton-swinging police, attacking German shepherd dogs, and a sad story about a church bombing that killed some little girls. I said, "Thanks, but I don't think that I'd be a good fit."

Brian was silent for a moment, then said, "Have you ever been to Birmingham?"

"Nope" I replied, "but in 1961 my parents and I visited my brother in Biloxi, Mississippi, after he joined the Air Force. It was my first exposure to 'White Only' restrooms, water fountains, and the like. That's really not my thing, Brian."

Once again he remained momentarily silent, as if letting my views of the south sink in. Then he said, "Well, you know, Tom, that was thirty years ago and things have really changed in the South. You owe it to yourself to come down and take a look around. We'll set you up in a first class hotel, a rental car, and all other expenses fully paid. Think of it as a paid mini-vacation to investigate the 'New South.' Just meet with the guys at the paper and see what they have to offer. Should you decide that Birmingham is not for you, there will be no hard feelings."

He was right. I was judging the place based solely on preconceived notions and thirty-year-old information. Maybe the time had come to take a fresh look at Dixie.

Touring

In 1991, the Birmingham airport was in dire need of a renovation. I actually got off the plane on the tarmac and had to walk up steps into the airport building. It was certainly not a great first impression.

I got the rental car and a map, and thus began my "mini-vacation." I drove first into downtown Birmingham to see where the newspaper buildings were located. The office building appeared to be very old, but directly behind it was a newer building that housed their offset presses. Other than a couple of newer bank towers, the remainder of the downtown area consisted of old buildings with a great many empty storefronts. After seeing the airport and now the downtown area, I was not feeling very positive or optimistic.

After investigating downtown, I drove up a hill and discovered a place called Five Points. It was a modest entertainment district consisting of some retail stores, restaurants, and a very odd-looking fountain with animal sculptures. One sculpture had a man's body with a horned animal head. It looked just a little satanic to me. But this area was lively and looked to be fun. My spirits rose a little.

I backtracked downtown in order to get on Hwy. 280 South. According to the map, that road led "over the mountain" to an area called Mountain Brook. I should mention that "over the mountain" is a local term referring to the developments on the other side of Red Mountain. That mountain, at least back then, was like a dividing line between the poor city and Mountain Brook's "old money," magnificent mansions and private country clubs. Red mountain also is the home to Vulcan—the largest cast iron statue in the world. The gigantic figure of the Greek god of fire and forge overlooks the city from atop the mountain and is a symbol of Birmingham's iron ore origins. The city was once called the Pittsburgh of the South due to its many steel mills and mining operations that employed thousands. Back then, it was also known as the Magic City due to its rapid population growth.

So I drove through the wooded hills of Mountain Brook marveling at the beautiful old homes that were set back from the narrow winding roads. *Now this is impressive*, I thought to myself. *There is some serious money in this town.* I also thought, *I bet this is where the publisher and the general manager of the newspaper live.*

Driving further south and then west, I discovered some of the newer developments in Hoover and Vestavia Hills. I came upon the Riverchase Galleria—a stunning mall with the Wynfrey Hotel tower on one side and an office tower on the other. *Brilliant*, I thought. *The mall has created a built-in shopper's base.* I continued on and drove through several subdivisions with newer homes. Much like Mountain Brook, the roads were narrow and winding with the homes built on heavily wooded lots.

As I drove around gawking at the houses and nicely landscaped yards, I was struck by the lack of people outside on this beautiful, sunny Saturday. The temperature was in the mid-to-high seventies, yet there were no kids outside playing, no moms lying in the sun, or dads washing cars or cutting grass. It just seemed odd. Where was everybody? When you got a day like this in Minnesota, nobody stayed inside. In fact, people tended to run around half naked. Maybe you had to experience a Minnesota winter in order to really appreciate springtime warmth. But I'll say this, I was very impressed with "over the mountain."

My Hotel

As my hotel, the Redmont, was located downtown, I headed back toward Birmingham via Hwy. 31 (Montgomery Highway). That road is a continuous ribbon of retail stores and car dealerships for much of the drive from Hoover to downtown Birmingham.

The Redmont is a beautiful and historic, old hotel. My issue was not with the hotel, but rather its location. There was nothing open around it, plus I didn't know the city or its high-crime areas. I didn't know if wandering the streets at night was safe, so I decided to be cautious and not venture out after dinner. I stayed in my room, watched TV, and pondered living in the South. I would have preferred staying at the Wynfrey in Hoover where I could have roamed around the mall after eating.

I Meet the Victors

Monday morning I headed over to the newspaper. I was currently the vice president of advertising at the *St. Paul Pioneer Press* and interviewing for the position of director of sales and marketing at the *Birmingham News*. I first met with the general manager of the paper, a very friendly young man in his mid-thirties named Victor Hansen III. He was slender, fit looking, and had a quick welcoming smile. He was a high-energy guy, to be sure, but there was a nervous edge about him that made me a little uncomfortable. As we talked, he seemed more nervous about the interview than I did. I couldn't help but wonder how such a young man was already the GM of a mid-size market metro daily. After chatting for an hour or so, he bounced up and said, "Let me give you a tour of the facilities." Hmmm—was the interview already over?

Leading me from floor to floor via the back stairs, I followed as he bounded up two steps at a time. I was a runner and in good shape, but I had a hell of a time keeping up with him. During the tour I met the division executives: the editor and the directors of circulation, production, and finance. They were all warm and personable and seemed knowledgeable. I'd often heard about southern hospitality, but so far my reception far exceeded all of my expectations.

As it approached noon, Victor told me that we would be having lunch at the Highlands Bar & Grill. It turned out that this very popular upscale restaurant wasn't all that far from the Five Points area I had discovered. *(Just a quick side bar: I recently read on the Internet that some organization or another had named the Highlands Bar & Grill the best restaurant in Alabama).* We were seated, and I noticed that the table was set for three. Victor then told me that the publisher was going to be joining us—a Mr. Victor Hanson II. Ah, now the pieces were falling into place!

My twenty-five years in the newspaper business afforded me the opportunity to meet literally thousands of people while making presentations and sales calls. I had worked with every type of business, business owner or manager, as well as many of their employees. I sold the St. Paul market and the benefits of advertising in the *St. Paul Dispatch* and *Pioneer Press* to accounts ranging from little mom-and-pop operations to large chain stores. I had worked with every conceivable type of personality, from the self-important demanding tyrants to the warm, pleasant, and appreciative individuals. Some of my customers were unsophisticated and possessed little business savvy while others absolutely blew me away with their brilliance. Several of my accounts wanted to hire me—others took out their frustration on me. I actually had one customer (a furrier) point a loaded pistol at me because he was very angry about the page on which his ad had appeared (thankfully his wife walked in possibly preventing a homicide).

My point is, I had been exposed to a great many personalities and styles. I became very astute at reading people and determining their personality type and their management style almost instantaneously. Yes, I tended to jump to conclusions based on first impressions, but I was rarely wrong.

The publisher arrived, looked around the restaurant, and then came charging over like a bull. Victor II was a heavy-set bald man in his late fifties or early sixties. After just a few minutes with him, I concluded that (1) He had grown up in a wealthy family, (2) He was very domineering, (3) He did not tolerate contradiction, and (4) He had a short fuse that frequently triggered an explosive temper. Turns out I was dead on. But for now, he was being nice and making friendly small talk. He asked several questions about my trip down, the hotel, and my family; but there were no questions at all regarding my qualifications for the position. He had delegated the "job interviewing" to Victor III.

After lunch, Victor III and I went back to his office. He excused himself and disappeared for a few minutes while I sat and waited. When he returned, he told me that he just had spoken with the publisher *(I found it interesting that he did not say with my dad or with my father)* and they had decided to invite me back. On the return trip he wanted to meet my wife and have her tour Birmingham in person. Same deal: airfare, hotel, rental car, meals, and miscellaneous expenses all covered. That certainly sounded like a "buying signal" to me. I agreed to another free mini-vacation…this one with Susie. I made one request: "Would you mind if we stayed at the Wynfrey rather than the Redmont?" He said, "That would be fine."

Two weeks later, on a Friday morning, Susie and I flew into Birmingham. I drove her around all the areas that I had discovered on my previous visit, and she seemed both excited and pleased with what she saw. Saturday night would be our only visit with the Hansens—just Victor III and his wife Mary. We had a wonderful dinner with them, and when dropping us off at the Wynfrey, he said, "You'll be hearing from me." Both Susie and I felt that sounded like the job would be mine if I wanted it. We talked it over and con-cluded that this opportunity was just too good to pass up. No more winter—Birmingham would be a fun new place to live. On Sunday we drove around looking at houses.

Really?

A couple of weeks passed and I had heard nothing from Birmingham. Then one evening the phone rang at the house, and it was Victor III. He thanked me for my interest, but they had decided to hire a guy from California. It was like getting punched in the gut. Being rejected after all that hurt like hell. I was not only disap-pointed, but I felt I had been misled and even betrayed. Despite that, I forced myself to write a nice warm and fuzzy letter to Victor III. I said that while this disappointment had left a bruise on my ego the size of a Buick, I was most appreciative to have been given the oppor-tunity to interview. I thanked him for his time, his kindness, and his generosity and concluded by wishing him, and his new hire, well. That letter turned out to be a very good idea. Never burn bridges.

Several months later, much to my surprise, Brian called me again from Atlanta. "Hey, Tom, guess what—Victor would like to talk to you about coming to Birmingham."

"Really?" I said. "What happened to that guy from California?"

"Well, let's just say that things didn't work out. Are you interested?"

I thought for a second and said, "Okay, Brian, how many other guys are interviewing this time?"

He said, "Nobody else... Victor wants you."

"That's nice," I said. "Let me talk it over with my wife, and I'll get back to you."

Susie and I were headed to Hayes, Kansas, to attend my niece Donna's wedding. I had told Brian that I'd call Victor along the way (which turned out to be from a hotel lobby in Topeka). When I called I was loaded for bear. I had everything written down: my desired salary, signing bonus, moving expenses, temporary housing, car allowance, paid vacation and trips back to Minnesota to sell the house and visit relatives. We had decided that if Victor wanted me, he could have me—but I wouldn't come cheap.

Much to my surprise, Victor, without any hesitation, agreed to everything that I requested, plus he even added a few things. I walked out of the hotel stunned. I got into the car where Susie had been patiently waiting and said, "We're movin' to Birmingham, y'all."

Farewell

My twenty-five-and-a-half-year career at the *St. Pioneer Press* was coming to an end. On Monday, September 30, 1991, I gave my two-week notice. I had not disappointed the man who had given me a chance—John Henry. I had in fact, risen from a rookie-classified rep with absolutely no sales experience to the highest position in the entire division. And, I might add, along the way, I requested to re-take that damn sales aptitude test. This time I scored 99 percent.

Just a few months before I gave my notice, John had decided to take an early retirement. At the dinner in his honor, he gave a wonderful farewell address in which he recounted his many memories and he thanked a lot of people by name. Then he looked at me sitting at one of the banquet tables and said, "Tom, you were my first hire, and you were my best hire." WOW—I felt so proud. My persistence, and his willingness to take a chance, had paid off for both of us.

The New Job

The plane from the Twin Cities to Birmingham (via Memphis) taxied to the terminal at about 10:00 a.m. on Saturday, October 12, 1991. I had left behind beautiful weather, but the fall colors were mostly gone. The leaves had already fallen to the ground. But here in the south, the gorgeous colors remained. I got to celebrate fall twice! As promised, a rental car was waiting for me at the airport. I followed the directions that were provided to an apartment complex in the residential community of Cahaba Heights. I would be living temporarily in a furnished apartment that was located just south of fashionable Mountain Brook.

The one-bedroom apartment was nice and looked clean, but I was going to make sure it was "sanitized." So off I went to the nearest grocery store where I stocked up on various cleaners, disinfectants, and paper towels. Back at the apartment I cleaned everything and then finally unpacked my suitcases. It was exhilarating yet somewhat frightening to be all alone in a strange city, in a strange apartment, driving a strange car and heading for a brand-new job where the last couple of guys "hadn't worked out." Oh, I don't mean "strange," so much as new and different. Regarding the new job, I wondered, *Would I work out?*

The Birmingham News

On Monday, October 14, I showed up at the office a little early and noticed that Victor II's BMW and Victor III's Buick were already parked in their reserved parking places. Those were the only two reserved parking places that were "posted," meaning name signs affixed to the wall. They were located right by the steps leading to the front door. Now to me, those parking spaces should have been reserved for customers, but I soon learned that things didn't work that way here. The rest of the parking lot adjacent to the office building was for supervisors, managers, and executives, which included me; but the spaces weren't assigned. The rank and file worker bees either parked in the lot across the street or in the parking ramp (sorry, parking DECK) next door.

I went in through the front doors and was directed to the personnel dept. There I filled out various forms, got a photo ID badge, was given a pile of brochures regarding company policies, then escorted to Victor III's office. Victor made small talk about my trip down, the apartment, etc., then said that my first order of business was to get a car. He made it quite clear that he expected me to drive a luxury car and that my $600-per-month car allowance should allow me to do just that. The car allowance was paid monthly with a separate check, and it would be $600 regardless of how much I was actually paying for a car. I told Victor I had been driving a company car for many years and that my last one was a new Lincoln Town Car. He said, "Great—get one of those." I told him that as much as I enjoyed driving around in a living room, I preferred something just a little smaller—like the Lincoln Continental. That was what I intended to look at, and he seemed pleased.

I was escorted into the advertising department where my new office was located. The entire building was old, and I thought a little depressing. After a tour of the various departments (classified, retail, creative, etc.) and the proper introductions had been made, I was led to my new office. Before entering, however, there was one more person to meet, my secretary Robyn Turner. She was stunning: mid-thirties, blond hair, blue eyes, trim figure, a beautiful warm smile, and when she spoke, it was with a soft Southern drawl. Welcome to Dixie.

One wall of the office faced the department's main hallway and the upper half was all glass. That meant that everybody that walked by could look in to see the new guy and probably wonder if he would last any longer than the previous two who had held the position.

Harris Emmerson was the senior manager in the advertising division in more ways than one. He had been at the paper a very long time, was in his seventies, and he not only knew all our advertisers, he knew most of their daddies too. While he was ultimately responsible for the performance and revenue production, it quickly became apparent that he and the number 2 guy, Bill Ward, *jointly* made all the decisions and recommendations.

Bill, a former Sears executive, was a stocky man in his fifties. He was the "inside man," meaning he took care of running the office and division sales structures. He was high energy, very assertive, opinionated, fast talking, knowledgeable, and savvy. Oh, there was also a most refreshing sense of humor. As time went on, he became one of my most favorite people of all time. I absolutely loved the guy.

Harris was the "outside man"—and the ultimate goodwill ambassador for the ad department and the entire newspaper. Everybody at the newspaper and in the community thought highly of Harris and I could easily see why…he was a warmhearted, good-natured, true Southern gentleman. He smiled nearly all of the time. I loved him as well.

Car Shopping

About midmorning Harris walked into my office and said, "I heard you wanted to go car shopping" (he had obviously been talking to Victor III). I said yes, and I was particularly interested in a new Lincoln Continental. He said, "Let's go—the owner of the Ford-Lincoln dealership is a friend of mine, and he'll give you a really good deal if I'm there with you." So off we went in my rental car—Harris riding shotgun and giving me directions along the way.

Someone must have called the dealership before we arrived because waiting for us at the front door was the owner and the general manager. After some pleasantries, they introduced me to a salesman who took me out onto the lot to look at Continentals. I found one in a color that I liked, and while Harris waited behind, we took it out for a test drive. I loved it and was ready to buy.

Back inside the showroom I caught up with Harris and told him of my decision to buy a new 1992 Continental. He didn't say anything at first but finally said, "The car you should really buy is that one right over there." I looked around and saw a jet black Lincoln Mark VII LSC Special Edition. It was a 1991 closeout model on which most of the trim, including the bumpers, was also black. The only chrome was that Rolls Royce style front grill, the wheels, and a thin strip on the sides. It also had that distinctive "Mark" series spare tire bump on the trunk. Because it was a sporty two-door, the doors were massive so passengers could access the back seat. I climbed in and fell in love with the luxurious leather interior, the comfortable bucket seats, the dashboard design, and the center console that was equipped with **a telephone**. I'd never even seen a car with a phone before.

The salesman wandered over and said, "I can give you a great deal on this one—it's our last Mark in stock." He then explained that the car was designed and equipped to compete with Audi, Mercedes, BMW, and the like. It had every conceivable option including Lincoln's most powerful V8 engine, racing suspension that provided a little stiffer ride but made it possible to corner at high speeds, and on and on. "Want to drive it?" he asked. "Absolutely," I responded.

He left and then returned with the keys. He hopped in, turned the key, and we heard "click-click-click." Uh-oh, it had a dead battery. I wondered if all those fancy electronic options were such a hot idea. He popped the hood, and then disappeared. A service area mechanic came in carrying a fresh battery, and we were soon on our way. Compared to other cars that I had driven, this one handled more like a sports car. That powerful engine combined with the rear wheel drive made it possible to "lay rubber" …just like in the good old days.

It wasn't exactly a "family car," but I knew that I'd be the only driver as Susie had her own car—a Honda Accord Hatchback. I tried, but failed, to hide the fact that I absolutely loved that car. You never want a car salesman see you drool. He said, "Well, what do you think? It's all yours for $28,000." The words, "I'll take it," flew out of my mouth before my brain had time to comprehend the price *(nearly twice what we paid for our first house)*.

Harris drove the rental car to the airport return area while I followed in my new Lincoln. Then we headed back to the newspaper. Soon Victor III had heard about my purchase and asked that I show it to him. What would he think of my new executive car? Keep in mind that he was a VERY conservative young man who drove a Buick Park Avenue four-door. We walked outside, and he closely inspected the *"Batmobile"* without saying a word. Then he finally said that he liked it. I don't know that he really did, but as he requested, I had gotten a "luxury" car. I'll explain calling it the *"Batmobile"* in just a bit.

"The Batmobile" 1991 Lincoln Mark VII LSC Special Edition. The nicest car I've ever owned

It was definitely a unique and highly recognizable car. In the two and one half years that I lived in Birmingham, I never saw another like it. It soon became closely associated with me, and people who knew me instinctively waved when they saw it. That was both good and bad…nice that I was recognized, bad in that there would be no getting around Birmingham incognito!

Back Home

On Friday, October 25, I flew back to Minnesota. I had already sold our beloved pontoon boat to a family that lived on the north side of First Lake. I stood on the dock watching as it was driven away. It was like losing a good friend. Susie's sister and brother-in-law bought the speed boat and moved it to the cabin up on Sugar Lake.

While home for the weekend, I needed to get that very expensive aluminum dock out of the water. We had decided to package both the dock and the pool table with the house as incentives. The weather was unusually warm—sunny and in the seventies. It was perfect for raking leaves, cutting grass, and pulling the dock. I worked all day Saturday knowing that I had to fly out Sunday afternoon. Susie and I agreed that she'd lock the place up and drive down to Birmingham the following weekend.

Winter Arrives Early

Halloween fell on a Thursday and Susie had planned to head for Birmingham the following day. That Halloween morning the rain quickly turned into freezing rain. As the temperature continued to drop and the wind picked up, it turned into heavy, wet snow and then a full-fledged blizzard. When it finally stopped late Friday afternoon, eighteen inches of snow lay on the ground with drifts over five feet high. Many roads were impassable, and there were accidents reported everywhere. Not only did the storm bury the Twin Cities, it also hit Wisconsin and Illinois—the very route needed to get from the Twin Cities to Birmingham.

Susie was trapped—she couldn't even get out of our long drive-way as it had drifted over. She called the guy who normally plowed for us and explained her dilemma. He made it over with chains on his truck and cleared the driveway but the roads remained in very bad shape. She then called our youngest son, Tom Jr., and he some-how made it over. That must have been quite a thrill ride. He said, *Let's finish loading your car, Mom. I'll drive you down to Birmingham."* Tom told me that the drive on I-94 in Minnesota and Wisconsin was white knuckle all the way. Illinois wasn't much better. They didn't see dry land until they were approaching the Kentucky border.

Tom stayed at a Birmingham area hotel and then flew back to Minnesota. Susie, meanwhile, was with me at the apartment and was certainly surprised by my choice of automobile!

Home Hunting

Always the helpful host, Victor III set us up with a local realtor friend who had a number of listings to show us. One of the very first homes was really off-the-beaten path. In fact, unless you knew about this new Vestavia Hills subdivision, you'd never know it even existed. She drove us down a narrow tree-lined side street that had mostly large single-story older homes. We then turned left onto a road that curved sharply as it went down a very steep hill. As we approached the bottom of the hill a brand-new subdivision emerged. About twenty-five beautiful two-story brick homes on one-acre lots filled the valley. And there, right on the corner at the base of the hill, was a new home still under construction. It was being built by Don Acton and listed through his in-house real estate company, Cornerstone Properties. The exterior brick was a very different color—almost a pink. The huge front yard had a sweeping circular driveway. In the rear, the lot seemed to go back forever. It ended in dense woods that rose up and over a steep hill. On the other side of that hill, well out of eyesight, lay I-459. Standing in back you could hear a little traffic noise, but it wasn't too bad. Because nothing could ever be built back there, the yard offered complete privacy. We'd miss lake living, but this home and property certainly had a lot of appeal.

Cornerstone Properties
Real Estate, Inc.
2232 Cahaba Valley Drive
Birmingham, Alabama 35242

SALES • CONSTRUCTION
RESIDENTIAL • COMMERCIAL

AREA CODE 205
TELEPHONE 991-9550

information deemed reliable but not guaranteed

WELCOME TO

2401 Altaridge Circle

Lot 14 - Altadena Ridge Estates

Lot Size - 288/316/310

This lovely 1½ story brick home has 4 bedrooms, 3½ baths, living room, dining room, den, kitchen with sun room and 2 car garage in full basement that is stubbed in for a bath. This is one of the two remaining new homes left in exclusive Altadena Ridge Estates in Vestavia Hills. The schools are Vestavia Hills Elementary-West, Pizitz Middle School and Vestavia Hills High School.

On the left side of the house, the circular drive connected with the driveway that led down to the basement level and the tuck under three-car garage. The home itself was nearly four thousand square feet with four bedrooms, an art/hobby studio with two skylights, three and a half baths, formal living room and dining room, a huge kitchen with a dine-in sunroom, arched doorways, and a beautiful staircase with a landing. Should we decide that we needed even more room, it had a semi-finished walk-out basement. Just as with buying the Lincoln, I blurted out, "We'll take it." The realtor looked stunned, not to mention the look on Susie's face. Say what? Susie was clearly searching for words. She finally said, "We don't need a house this big for just the two of us." Need? No. I didn't **need** a hot rod Lincoln either. This was not a case of NEED…this was a case of WANT.

The realtor said, "Well, unfortunately this particular house has been sold to a couple moving here from Atlanta." I said, "I didn't see a sold sign in front."

She said that they hadn't actually signed any paperwork yet because they wanted pricing on some change orders first. That being the case, at least to my way of thinking, it was only a non-binding verbal commitment. I said, "Then it's still for sale—call the builder."

Susie loved the house but thought it was too large, too pretentious, and too expensive. I countered with, "You only move to Birmingham once." A lot of things had to happen in order for us to get the house, but we got it and moved in shortly before Thanksgiving. *If that couple from Atlanta happens to be reading this, I do apologize for stealing your house.* Because all our household goods were still up in Forest Lake, we rented a bed, some living room furniture, and then bought a new TV. Before anything was even shipped down from Minnesota, we started shopping for some new furniture to fill this huge house. Wow—new city, new job, new car, and now a new house. Things were moving fast in Birmingham.

Each morning I'd head down the basement steps and into the garage where my beautiful black Lincoln was parked. I'd frequently back the car into the garage so that I had a clear shot out in the morning. I'd hit the garage door opener button, and zoom out and straight up that steep driveway. That's when it hit me…it was like Batman pulling out of the Bat cave. Thus, my nickname for the car, *The Batmobile.*

Getting Involved

We flew back to Minnesota for Christmas. Before we arrived, our three grown sons had gone over and completely decorated the house for Christmas—including putting up the tree. What a wonderful surprise. We enjoyed one last Christmas together on the lake.

A couple of months later the house sold. As we had already purchased a lot of new furniture and décor in Birmingham, we gave the boys quite a bit of stuff. We then arranged to have the rest moved down.

Meanwhile, back at the paper, Victor III made it clear that I was to be the out front person for the paper. "Get involved," I was told. So I got involved: Birmingham Executive Institute, Chamber of Commerce Board, Downtown Council Board, Broadway Series Board, Sales and Mktg. Executives Board, United Way, etc. I was EVERYWHERE. And my job was going great. So pleased were the Victor's that they gave me a 12.5 percent salary increase on my first anniversary. On my second anniversary, October 14, 1993, I received a note from the publisher which read in part: "I can't believe you've been here two years today. The breath of fresh air and creativity you have brought to our advertising and sales efforts has meant so much. Thanks for your valuable contribution and friendship." And I was given even more money—but in just five weeks I'd be fired.

What Did I Expect?

The excitement of the move, the success on the job, the involvement in the community, and all things "new" couldn't mask the strain on our marriage. Things had not been going well for quite some time, and Susie and I had even discussed a separation while still living in Minnesota. I actually went out looking at apartments, but I just couldn't bring myself to go through with it.

Susie has a couple of expressions that she uses quite frequently: if she *agrees* with someone and likes what she is hearing, you can count on her to say "yah"—often many times in the course of a conversation. I used to hear "yah" a lot when she was talking on the phone. I guess that's a Minnesota Scandinavian thing. If she *disagrees* with something or is offended by what she hears, her comment is usually, "Oh, brother." Depending on the circumstances, it can be said quite sarcastically. In those instances, that phrase also comes with an eye roll. I was getting a lot more "oh, brothers" than "yahs."

I guess we both had thought that the move to Birmingham would bring us closer together, and for a while it did. But once again, we were drifting apart. She had changed so much that I hardly knew how to act around her. So many things seemed to offend her.

I had begun to enjoy listening to country music. I particularly liked "new" country as some of it came with a driving drum-and-guitar beat that was reminiscent of old time rock and roll. I really liked the harmony and music of Alabama, but I absolutely loved a brand-new duo called Brooks & Dunn. I had heard their new song a couple of times and thought it was fantastic. Well, Susie and I were returning home from somewhere, and as I pulled into our driveway, that new Brooks & Dunn song came on the radio. I cranked up the volume and said, "This is really great." The lyrics to "Born to Love Again" begin:

> I *saw the light*
> *I've been baptized*
> *By the fire in your touch*
> *And the flame in your eyes*
> *I'm born to love again*
> *I'm a brand new man*

I heard, "Oh, brother," saw the eye roll, and she got out. Apparently, she felt that those words trivialized the Christian "born-again" experience. That honestly had never even crossed my mind.

I had hoped our new life in Dixie would somehow decrease her religious intensity. Why, I don't know. After all, we had moved to the *buckle of the Bible belt*. After joining Briarwood Presbyterian church, she made new friends with fervor similar to her own. While I did accompany her to Sunday services and actually liked many of the sermons, I was really in it for the breakfasts that we'd enjoy afterwards at the Vestavia Hills Country Club. Unlike Forest Hills golf club, this place sat on top of a mountain, it was ELEGANT, and the food was fantastic.

Looking back, maybe it was just my imagination, but I felt that I was constantly being judged. It was like every word and action was being scrutinized. I even felt guilty mixing a cocktail when I got home from work. You know, you shouldn't feel uncomfortable in your own home.

One evening, as I arrived home from work, I noticed that a black Mercedes was parked in the circular drive by our front door. I had no idea whose car that was—I had never seen it before. I parked in the "Bat cave" and went up the stairs and into the kitchen. Susie was there along with two couples that I had never met. I was introduced and told they were friends from our church. I offered to mix them a drink, but they politely declined. So I went ahead and mixed myself one.

As it turned out, it was a "religious intervention" and apparently Susie's last-ditch effort to save my sorry ass. These folks were here at her request, and they urged me to get down on my knees, confess my sins, and accept the Lord into my life. They would witness this transformation (miracle?) and welcome me into the fold. I invited them to leave.

Let's just say that incident didn't help our failing marriage. I was angry; and she was disappointed, hurt, and a little indignant. After all, she had only been trying to lead her husband into what she viewed as certain salvation. A well-intentioned objective to be sure, but I was not yet ready to be led. I think at that point we both realized that our twenty-eight-year marriage was in serious trouble. Separation and even divorce crossed my mind. I'm sure it crossed hers as well.

The End of Two Marriages

Now here's an interesting coincidence: I confided to my executive assistant, Robyn, that my marriage was in trouble. She, in turn, told me that her marriage was also on the rocks. After that frank discussion, we often talked about our failing relationships and how difficult it was dealing with them. It was much worse for her because she had two young children. Things eventually reached the breaking point for her and her husband, Jerry, and he moved out and into an apartment. Before long, I ended up doing the same.

Susie was now all alone in that big house, and I was trying to get used to a small one-bedroom apartment with rented furniture. Tom and Susie and Robyn and Jerry were all headed to divorce court. But let me state unequivocally that Susie had always been a wonderful wife, a terrific mother, and, currently, an extraordinary grandma. I've loved her since the seventh grade, and I continue to do so to this very day. I would never, ever, do anything to hurt her. She had to go down the path that she believed was right for her. To do anything else would have been hypocritical. The same, however, was true for me.

Romance Blossoms

Robyn was not only attractive, she was smart, good-natured, funny, creative, organized, and pretty darn talented. From a professional standpoint, she could keep up with my rapid fire Yankee dictation with her shorthand skills (now a lost art).She typed in excess of one hundred words per minute, and she kept me organized, on time, and on track. It also didn't hurt that she appreciated my slightly offbeat sense of humor. I truly enjoyed making her laugh. I simply couldn't have asked for a more efficient assistant. But she was becoming more than my assistant; she was becoming my partner. I bounced everything off her and welcomed her ideas, advice, and input. We began having lunch together several times a week to discuss new ideas, new programs and concepts, staff structure, job responsibilities, etc. I trusted her judgment and always felt safe in discussing even the most confidential and sensitive of matters with her.

We never tried to hide our luncheons—I'd pull right up to the front door of the paper, and she'd come out and climb into my car. We didn't care who saw that—after all, it was just another business lunch—until it wasn't.

One day Robyn and I had lunch at the Brookwood Village Mall. As usual, it was a fun lunch. We talked non-stop and paused only to laugh about one thing or another. It was clear that we truly enjoyed each other's company. After lunch we walked out into the bright sunshine and to the Batmobile. Once inside, something just happened. We looked at each other and then bent over the center console and kissed. Just one kiss. Then we drove back to the newspaper in complete silence—both trying to come to grips with what had just happened. Things were very awkward between us the rest of the afternoon.

The next morning she came into my office and said she thought it would be best if she turned in her resignation. Clearly she was feeling guilty, and maybe even ashamed, of what had happened. She wanted to run away—a trait I later learned was her way of dealing with most problems. I literally begged her to stay and promised her that our relationship henceforth would be strictly professional. Yeah, right. Like that was going to happen.

Birmingham Becomes the Arctic Circle

It was Friday, March 12, 1993, and the warm temperatures and sunshine of that morning were predicted to give way to what could develop into a major snowstorm. Lots of moisture was moving up from the Gulf while a huge Canadian cold front was moving down from the north. The collision was expected to occur that evening right on top of Birmingham. Victor III had a number of rooms reserved at the Radisson Hotel near Five Points, just in case things got really bad. He asked that I, and several other key managers, spend the evening at the hotel. We were then instructed to go home and pack for the overnight stay. While we would be at the hotel, and presumably at the newspaper the next day, he and the publisher would weather the storm in their Mountain Brook homes.

By mid-afternoon, the sunshine had given way to rain. Early that evening, the rain turned to snow. We had all left our cars in the newspaper parking lot and been given a ride to the hotel in a company truck. The driver said he'd return in the morning to take us back to the newspaper. He also mentioned he was headed to the garage to install tire chains. That seemed wise.

Around six thirty that evening, the four of us met in the lobby and decided to walk the six or so blocks up to Five Points to eat.

We trudged up the hill through the snow and found that only one restaurant remained open—a pizza place. We sat at a table by the windows, ate pizza, and watched the snowstorm intensify. They kidded me about being from Minnesota and probably responsible for dragging this weather down from the hinterlands. We walked back in four or five inches of snow, and I thought "no big deal by Minnesota standards"…but that was about to change.

In the morning, I went down to the lobby for breakfast. I was shocked to see people everywhere. Many were sleeping on the lobby furniture, others on the floor. The storm had gotten so bad over night that people had to be rescued from the interstates. Hotels and motels were completely booked, so people slept wherever they could find a warm place to lay their heads. While all this was going on, I was sleeping in my large comfy room with two queen beds and these people were sleeping on the floor.

We called the newspaper, and the truck eventually arrived. Driving was very difficult even with chains on the truck tires. A lot more snow was predicted as the day wore on. There was already about a foot of snow on the ground, and they were saying that a total of eighteen inches or more was possible. By dinner time the snow had stopped with a total accumulation of seventeen inches. This would have been considered a big storm by Midwestern standards, but in Birmingham, Alabama, it was HISTORIC. It would become known as *the Storm of the Century*. Saturday evening, even the truck with chains couldn't move. We had eaten out of vending machines all day, so we agreed to walk in the middle of the un-plowed streets to the Redmont Hotel for dinner. After a nice hot dinner (and a cocktail or two) we navigated through the downtown area and back to the Radisson.

The weight of the snow brought down a lot of trees—especially the tall southern pines that had a shallow root system. Trees blocked roads and lay across roofs all over the city. Many parts of Birmingham and the surrounding communities were without power. Transformers exploded and power lines snapped under the weight of the wet heavy snow or the falling trees.

For most homes, no power meant no heat. Susie was home alone in a big cold house. For some warmth, she hung sheets and blankets across the family room doorways and kept the gas fireplace turned on. Right outside the family room door was a gas grill she could use to cook some meals. It was fueled by a natural gas line rather than a propane tank, so she did not have to worry about running out of fuel—only running out of food.

She'd bundle up, dash out, put something on the grill, and then dash back in while it cooked. She was trapped, and I was unable to reach her as all the roads in the area were completely blocked by dozens of downed trees. Besides, my car was buried under a foot and a half of ice and snow.

The road conditions also prevented emergency vehicles from operating. In fact, an L-shaped shopping center burned completely to the ground as fire trucks were unable to get anywhere near it. Included in that center was a comedy club and all of comedian Carrot Top's props were burned to a crisp. As the city had no snowplows, they used road graders in an effort to clear the main arteries that weren't blocked by fallen trees, power poles, or electrical lines.

The temperatures began to rise on Sunday, Monday, and Tuesday. The snow melted quickly, but the tree and power line problems persisted for many days. I finally made it back to the house Tuesday afternoon, sprung Susie from her frigid prison and to the warmth of the hotel. I doubt that she had been that cold since our honeymoon. Well, that doesn't sound good, does it? You know darn well that I'm referring to the chairlift incident.

Robyn and Jerry had gotten divorced, but Sue and I continued to be married even though we were living apart. I began seeing Robyn after work on occasion, but she had two children to care for, so it was not often. After a period of time, we finally admitted to ourselves, and to each other, that we were in love.

Painful Ordeal

I was living in a ground floor apartment of a brand-new complex in Cahaba Heights. In fact, it was not far from the temporary furnished apartment that I had lived in when I first arrived in town. I was the very first person to live in my unit, so it was nice and clean both inside and out. The place still smelled of fresh paint and new carpet. That is why I found it strange to suddenly find cigarette butts on and around my small concrete patio. I guessed they must be from some apartment complex workers. Then I began getting some strange phone calls nearly every evening. I'd answer, but there would be nobody there. Maybe somebody just kept dialing the wrong number, or possibly, it was someone checking to see if I was home. I had no idea, but it was certainly odd.

It was on the evening of Monday, November 22, 1993, and before leaving work, I walked down to Victor III's office to discuss a new promotional opportunity. After we chatted, he gave me permission to proceed with the project. As I headed for the door, I said, "Thanks, Victor, I'm a happy camper." He responded by saying, "I hope you're not staying home tonight." I thought that comment was strange, but I said nothing and just kept walking. Turns out, it had been a warning.

Robyn came over to my apartment that evening for dinner. The kids were with grandma and grandpa. I had purchased some salads from Jack's and opened a bottle of Kendall-Jackson chardonnay. While we were eating, the telephone rang. Once again nobody responded when I said "Hello." Later, I walked her out to the parking lot and to her car. Before she got in, I gave her a kiss good night along with a tight hug and said, "I love you. See you in the morning."

Tuesday morning, I arrived at the newspaper early and went directly to my office. Robyn had not yet arrived, and I was sitting at my desk when Bill Ward came rushing in and said, "Something is going on."

"What?" I asked.

"I don't know, but I saw the HR director in the parking lot, and she was carrying some large envelops. I said good morning, but she rushed right by me without saying a word. Then I saw her and Victor III go into the publisher's office."

Well, I knew that Bill had moles all over the building, so eventually, he'd get to the bottom of it.

I said, "Let me know what you learn."

He said that he would and left.

Around 10:00 a.m. Robyn came into my office and said that the publisher wanted to see me. *Odd*, I thought. He's usually heading to the YMCA to play racquetball about now.

I walked into Victor II's office, and Victor III was sitting in a side chair with several large envelopes on his lap. Looking as serious as a heart attack, the publisher said, "Sit down." He was red faced and clearly very upset. As soon as I sat down, he said, "We'll need your resignation effective immediately."

I said, "Why?"

It was then that Victor III spoke up.

Unlike his father, he wasn't angry, he just seemed sad.

"Have you been seeing Robyn Turner outside of work hours?"

I said. "On occasion."

He continued, "Was she at your apartment last evening?"

POW…it hit me like a flash. I knew exactly what was in those envelopes. They had hired a private detective, which explained the cigarette butts and mysterious phone calls. He must have been in the parking lot last evening snapping pictures. I felt sure that there was at least one showing me kissing Robyn. Get real—there were probably twenty of them. It had been a pretty long and passionate kiss. In fact, the guy may have run out of film. Then the odd statement that Victor III had made last night made sense: "I hope you're not staying home this evening."

I was trapped…they knew it, and I knew it. I must have had that deer-in-the-headlights look.

"Yes—she was there last night."

"Please leave the building immediately and come back after hours to clean out your desk," the publisher said harshly.

I just sat there in silence for a minute, then got up and left— totally devastated.

I drove over to the house and told Susie what had happened. She had known about Robyn for some time so that didn't come as a shock or a surprise. My firing sure did, though. I have long suspected, but never really known, if Susie may have inadvertently played a role in my demise. If she had confided to somebody at Briarwood about our separation and my on-going relationship with Robyn, that would certainly not sit well with the church elders. It would be particularly bad if the minister found out as he and the publisher were good friends. Victor II had been a long-time member of the congregation and a MAJOR church contributor. This situation would be most embarrassing for him, and he certainly would take it as a personal insult. That scenario made sense to me based on how angry he had been.

My world collapsed: the house went up for sale, the divorce papers were processed, and I was unemployed at age forty-eight. What on earth would I do now? I'll tell you this, I was VERY scared. But on the bright side, I had lasted longer than the previous two guys!

Chapter 7

Chapter 7

Goodbye Birmingham

After the house sold, Susie moved into an apartment. I helped her move, get settled, and even hung pictures for her. We were pleasant to each other, but I think we were both numb from the trauma of a divorce after twenty-eight years of marriage, the loss of my job, the sale of a home that we loved, and her apartment move. It was a lot happening at one time.

She continued her relationship with her friends at Briarwood and then got involved in an English teaching program. She assumed that I would be leaving the area and our oldest son Mike, who lived nearby, was constantly on the road for his job. She really had no reason to stay in Birmingham, so she decided to head back north to St. Paul. She rented an apartment there and continued her involvement in a program that teaches conversational English to Chinese. Well, that's the "cover" story…the real intent is to do missionary work. She attended a school for that program in San Francisco, and once trained, she was off to China where she would spend the better part of the next ten years. We did not have any contact during that period.

Resumes and Interviews

During my time at the *Birmingham News*, I had made a lot of friends as well as business and civic acquaintances. One top-notch lawyer friend even wanted to sue the newspaper on my behalf, but I was guilty and had left the Victors little choice but to let me go. The *Birmingham News* is a part of Advance Publications, a corporation privately owned by the Newhouse family. They avoid litigation like the plague and employ lots of lawyers—very good lawyers. The day before I was dismissed, Mark Newhouse had been in town. He met with me to discuss ad revenues and expenses and then afterwards with the Victors. I'm sure at that meeting my impending termination was discussed and that at least one of the corporate attorneys had been consulted. So a lawsuit would be unwise and possibly even be detrimental to my job search. Others in the community offered to help me by writing letters of introduction and recommendation. Those certainly proved to be beneficial.

Being an executive at a metro daily comes with one big downside—there is usually only one daily newspaper in town. That means that should you unexpectedly become unemployed, you either had to move to another market or change careers. At forty-eight years of age and an entire career in the newspaper industry, let's face it, I really only had one option—MOVE.

About a month before my termination, I had received a call from Russ Hunsaker, a Chicago recruiter, wondering if I might be interested in a position at the *Omaha World-Herald*. At the time, I was happily employed, making lots of money, and with no desire to return to the frigid north. I had told him, "No, thanks." If only I had had a crystal ball.

Lawler, Ballard, and Van Durand was the ad agency of record for the *Birmingham News*. I worked closely with them in the promotion of the newspaper through other media: TV, radio, outdoor, direct mail, etc. They also designed many of the promotion ads that appeared on the pages of the newspaper. The owner/president of that agency is Tinsley Van Durand. Upon hearing of my sudden departure from the newspaper, he called me at my apartment to offer his help. He suggested that I "office" out of his agency, where I'd have access to all his resource materials including the newspaper industry magazine *Editor & Publisher*. I was welcome to use their telephones and utilize their support staff for the typing and mailing of my resume and cover letters. I think we both realized that beyond just the help and resources that his operation would offer, it was also important for me to have some place to go each morning. I quickly accepted his most generous and kind invitation, and I continue to be grateful to him to this very day. He was there for me when I needed help, and that certainly meant a lot.

I had a good reputation within the newspaper industry, and over the years I had served on various newspaper association committees and boards including a stint as president of the Midwest Newspaper Advertising Executives Association. Now as a "free agent" I made use of all those connections by making a lot of telephone calls. In addition, I mailed out letters and resumes to those newspapers who had listed job opportunities in *Editor & Publisher*.

Because of the one town-one paper reality, the industry is really a small and tight-knit community. Keep in mind, many newspapers were, and continue to be, just parts of large publishing/communications companies. Back then some of the larger "chains" were Gannett, Tribune, Hearst, Knight-Ridder, Times-Mirror, and the privately held Newhouse empire. My sudden "availability" quickly spread throughout the industry.

Nothing happened over the holidays, which was expected, but nonetheless discouraging. The inactivity added to my anxiety. In mid-January 1994, I flew to interviews in Pittsburgh and Richmond. The position in Pittsburgh was interesting and offered advancement opportunities while the new media director job in Richmond was clearly out of my league. I am certainly no tech guy—I still use a flip-phone (well, so does Warren Buffet, so I'm in good company).

Omaha Comes Knocking Again

Then like a bolt out of the blue, I got another call from Russ, the *Omaha* headhunter. We chatted for a bit, and this time I expressed interest. He suggested that the next step would be for me to take a management aptitude test over the telephone. C'mon, I had twenty-eight years of success. Besides, I hated those damn things and discovered over the years that the folks who tended to do the best on them could be the worst "real world" performers. Conversely, those who scored low often became the stars.

When I was hiring, I never relied much on test results or fancy professionally written cover letters or inflated "blow smoke up your hoo-ha" resumes that included exaggerated educational honors or work experience. I liked the face-to-face interview where I could measure things like energy, job knowledge, management style, manners, ability to speak and think on their feet, and even check for a sense of humor. I loved the good old days when all job applications were handwritten and filled out in pen in the personnel department. From those, you could gage neatness, penmanship, spelling, grammar, and the ability to form a sentence (or convey a thought). After a while, you just got a "gut feel" and I had much better luck with that than with test scores.

Sorry, I got off on a tangent there. I guess the mere mention of "test" took me back to that first sales aptitude test that I had to take at the *Pioneer Press*. Based on that, I should have NEVER been hired.

Regardless of my personal feelings and experience, I had no choice but to agree to the testing. Later that day my phone rang and the nearly thirty-minute Q and A session began. There were endless "what-would-you-do" multiple-choice questions. In most cases, I would not have chosen any of the suggested answers. I knew how to handle problems and crises situations, create teamwork, handle difficult employees and customers, build consensus, run meetings, empower and motivate coworkers, hire and fire...and by god, I sure as hell knew how to grow revenues. I had successfully done so for nearly thirty years. So when they wanted to force me into choosing one of their answers, my frustration began to show. Yes, I got testy with the tester. I even said that many of their "canned classroom answers" were not only ill conceived...some were downright stupid. When I hung up I thought that would be the last that I'd hear from Omaha. It was too damn cold up there anyway!

A few days later Russ called again. "Hi, Tom, could you fly down to Dallas to meet with me?" *Hmmm*, I thought, *no mention of the test. Fly to Dallas for a job in Omaha. Is that something like fly to Atlanta for a job in Birmingham?* "Sure," I said.

I knew that candidates for this position were probably stacked up like cord wood. An employee-owned newspaper was a rarity, and the opportunity to actually own a piece of the action was very attractive. I hoped that my experience as the VP of advertising at a Midwest newspaper would give me an edge, but I had no idea who my competition was.

As with previous interviews in my life, this one with Russ seemed to go well. I can usually remain calm in stressful situations and frequently use humor to lighten the atmosphere. If I can't get somebody to laugh, then I know I'm in trouble. I got him to laugh. Over the years I annoyed some of my superiors with my humor approach. Many of them later ended up working for me—*how's that for funny?* Humor tends to loosen you up so you can relax, which, I believe, allows you to think more clearly, rationally, and strategically, than those serious uptight hand wringers.

About a week after my Dallas interview, Russ called with the following request: "Tom, they'd like you to fly up to Omaha for an interview and to meet with some of the executives." I said sure and a date was set. I flew in and checked into my room at a flea bag hotel near the airport. This place made most budget motels look pretty elegant. *(Okay, I'm exaggerating a bit.)* Bill Donaldson, the VP of sales, had set-up these wonderful accommodations. I later learned that he was known around the newspaper as "Dollar Bill" because he was, let's say, frugal.

He picked me up later that afternoon for a quick city tour and then dinner. Bill was in his early sixties and just a little gruff. I dug deep to find a sense of humor but came up dry. We drove around town and past the World-Herald Building but did not go in. That would wait until tomorrow. We ended up at a restaurant called Johnny's Cafe in South Omaha. It was an old-fashioned steak house that had been in operation next to the stockyards since 1922. The stockyards were long gone, but Johnny's continued to serve up great dinners generation after generation. *(It was later the site of Jack Nicholson's retirement dinner scene in the 2002 movie* About Schmidt.*)*

After dinner, Bill dropped me off at the Bates Motel. My room was the first one off the lobby. Between the jet noise at the airport, the lobby noise, and my fear that the cockroaches would climb into bed with me, I had a rough night. *(All right, there were no roaches that*

I know of.) As promised, Bill picked me up in the morning and we were off to the newspaper building where I got the usual tour and had brief meetings with all the key executives, except the publisher. I thought things had gone pretty well, but then again, I usually do.

Russ called a week later and said they wanted me back in Omaha. That seemed to be positive, but then I got the Birmingham flashback—the first visit went fine, the second visit was great—then I was rejected.

For this trip I requested to stay in West Omaha at the Marriott in Regency. They agreed to this extravagant request. What a contrast from the airport motel. I spent considerable time with Rick Seibert, the circulation director. I thought that to be somewhat strange until I learned that he was being considered for the general manager position. I had dinner that night with Rick and his wife Debbie. Both were very nice, and each had a delightful sense of humor, so the entire evening was light and quite enjoyable. The next morning I spent time with the publisher, John Gottschalk, who kept glancing at something on his desk. I suspected he may have been studying my "test" results. (Yeah, I was just a little paranoid.) He did most of the talking, and I did most of the listening...and that was just fine by me.

I was back in my Birmingham apartment when Russ finally called about a week later. He had an offer that included the salary, vacation, bonus structure, moving allowance, temporary housing, and stock opportunities. This offer had "Dollar Bill" written all over it. He was once again trying to save money by offering me the "*Bates Motel package,*" and I was determined to hold out for the "*Marriott package.*" I countered, and Russ acted shocked at what I was requesting. I said, "Well, run it by them. All they can say is no." He did not seem pleased but said that he'd get back to me. The next day he called with a little better offer, which I refused. I stood firm on my salary and paid vacation requests. And because it was an employee-owned operation, I asked that there be no limit on the number shares that I could purchase.

Russ was not only irritated, he also sounded frustrated. Then came the warning: "I've been doing this a long time, and I have to tell you, Tom, I think that your demands will annoy them to the point that they'll withdraw their offer and move on to another candidate." I then told Russ that I had another offer (pure bluff) and to let me know ASAP if they were going to pass. Within an hour my phone rang. They had agreed to my salary and vacation demands, but it was "no" regarding the stock. Russ told me that the publisher was the only person on the planet who determined how much stock any individual could purchase. I said, "Okay, Russ, tell them we have a deal." He was then my friend again. He said that I'd be hearing from Bill Donaldson but to expect that my first day would be Tuesday, March 1.

Hello Again, Winter

The weather in Birmingham had been unusually warm for February, so I didn't mind waiting a couple of weeks to start my new job. The house had sold quickly, and what home furnishings Sue hadn't taken, I moved into storage. I quite literally had nothing to do, so I laid poolside at the apartment complex and got a nice tan. As I had pre-paid my apartment rent through May, I could leave most everything behind and get it, and everything in the storage unit, moved to Omaha once I had a house to ship it to.

On Saturday, February 26, 1994, I loaded up the Batmobile, kissed Robyn good-bye, and headed north. I stayed overnight in Columbia, Missouri, and arrived in Omaha on Sunday, February 27. They had a nice large furnished apartment waiting for me. I unpacked and thought I could buy essentials, like food, the following day as I wasn't scheduled to start work until Tuesday. But Bill Donaldson had my apartment phone number, and he called me that evening. He wanted to know how my trip up had gone and could I actually start first thing in the morning. Sure, squeeze a "free day" out of the new guy, Dollar Bill.

Monday morning, I drove downtown and found snow piled up against the curbs everywhere. After spending the last couple of winters in the South, I was not looking forward to dealing with the snow and cold again. I parked at a meter and walked two blocks to World-Herald Square. I was once again in a personnel department completing forms and being issued a photo ID badge. I was told that Bill was in a meeting but would catch up with me soon. I was then escorted to my office where I met Carolyn, my administrative assistant, and discovered my desk was already stacked high with paperwork.

As I was sorting through the piles, Bill walked in, apologized for not being available when I had arrived, and officially welcomed me to the paper. Then I was presented with my first problem: "We've got a serious situation with a million-dollar national preprint advertiser. They've sent us a letter cancelling all future inserts in our paper and have decided to use direct mail instead. You will probably need to fly to New York to resolve this." Well, at least he hadn't said, "You'll have to take a *Greyhound bus* to New York to resolve this."

It was a new market but the same old problems. I was quite familiar with this customer and their threats and demands. "Okay, I'll get on it."

Could I Be Any Dumber?

The next weekend I bought a house. Nothing big and grandiose like Birmingham, but decent: the 2,500-square-foot house had four bedrooms, two and half baths, a three-car garage, and an unfinished walk-out basement. While it was a much smaller lot, it was also priced about half of the Birmingham house. Lower monthly payments were a must as I was now paying alimony.

15412 Lloyd Street, Pacific Hollow, Omaha, Nebraska

The house had been unoccupied, so after a quick closing, I was able to take immediate possession. That gave me the opportunity to start refurbishing it. The first project was peeling the wallpaper off the walls in the family room and the upstairs bath. One evening, I was working in the bathroom, kneeling in the tub peeling wallpaper, and for some dumb reason, I stood up quickly and hit the top of my forehead on the shower head (which was obviously positioned too low). I hit it hard, and there was blood running down my face. It was quite the gash, so I drove over to the hospital emergency room where I got a few stitches…my first since Jerry had pegged that snowball at me many years before. Nice timing—I was flying to New York the very next morning to meet with the guy who wrote that nasty letter.

Actually, the timing couldn't have been better!

The Big Apple

I'd never been to New York City before, and my first impression was a little like Gomer Pile "Gaaa-lee, look at all the tall buildings." I was booked into an okay hotel—nothing fancy, yet surprisingly expensive. After checking in, I walked around in the rain, getting constantly bumped by umbrella-wielding pedestrians. I moved my wallet from my back pocket to my front pocket as I'd been warned about pickpockets! Then I came upon a quaint little Italian restaurant where I enjoyed a wonderful pasta dinner and a couple glasses of Chianti. Then it was back to the hotel.

Thankfully, I didn't have to take a taxi the next morning. I had seen how the natives stepped right out into the street to hail a cab. I thought, being a novice, I'd probably just get run over. Anyway, I was able to walk from my hotel to the advertiser's office building.

Waiting for me in the reception area was a guy from the national rep firm. They represented us to national clients until there was a problem. They didn't handle problems. The concept of having a national rep firm represent you was to save on the travel budget. While their fees were not cheap, retaining them was less expensive than flying our own folks all over the country. His firm represented a lot of newspapers nationally, but today, he was there only for me and the *Omaha World-Herald*.

We were ushered into a large conference room where Irv, the top dog, sat along with three female associates. All four of them looked angry, and the introductions hadn't even made yet. Irv looked at my forehead and asked, "What happened to you?" My first thought, *Gain some sympathy. Tell them you had gotten mugged.* Instead, I told them about my impending marriage, the new house, and stripping wallpaper. I guess that "humanized" me as I sensed far less hostility in the room. They even shared a few remodeling stories of their own.

We discussed our ad insertion rates, and I finally made several pre-authorized rate concessions (which is all they were really after). They reinstated their business; so they seemed happy, I was happy, and our national sales rep also appeared to be happy. *(Well, I saw his teeth and assumed it was a smile. I guess it could have just been gas.)* We all went out to an honest to god New York deli for lunch. The food was great, and they even paid! We parted friends, and the trip turned out to be most rewarding. Flying out I decided that New York was just too tall and too crowded for this Minnesota boy. Back in Omaha, they were pleased that I was able to get the business reinstated. The head wound had certainly helped.

The Visit

I was so excited—Robyn was flying up for the weekend. It was April, but still cold. I picked her up at the airport, and we went to my apartment and got re-acquainted. We were then off to lunch, a tour of the city, and, lastly, my big surprise…the house. As we drove through the far western fringes of Omaha, still farm country at the time, the snowflakes began to fall. She got so excited—like a little girl. Looking over at her, I felt so good seeing that sheer joy on her face. It made me realize just how much I had missed her and how deeply I loved her.

Her bliss and my joy, however, were to be short-lived. I drove into Pacific Hollow, a subdivision just a mile or so west of the Boys

Town campus, and after a few turns, I pulled into the driveway of the house on Lloyd Street.

"What's this?" she asked.

"Our new home," I replied.

"WHAT? You bought a house without me?"

Yes, in retrospect, it was clearly the wrong thing to do. But, in my defense, she should have been used to me doing stupid things by now. We toured the house, and she liked it, but was understandably hurt that I had made this huge decision without including her. Honestly, as I look back, I ask myself how I could have been so insensitive and thoughtless? I have so many regrets.

The Omaha World-Herald

As I had done at the *Birmingham News*, my first order of business was to individually take each ad division supervisor and manager out to lunch. I let each choose the restaurant. Those one-on-one meetings gave me the opportunity to learn something about their personality, job responsibilities, management style, ambitions and, hopefully, without prying, a little about their personal lives. I also sought their advice: *"In your opinion, how can operations be improved?"* I quickly discovered that I had inherited a very good management team, plus, for the most part, an excellent and dedicated sales staff.

The two key managers, Diana Condon, the retail advertising manager, and Dale Harris, the classified advertising manager, were especially talented and both had been with the paper a long time. I had known, liked, and respected Dale from my days as the classified manager in St. Paul. We had become friends through the various conventions and conferences.

Diana became my "right-hand man." *(I know that's the wrong term, but you know what I mean.)* She was an excellent manager but had not been allowed to really blossom. My predecessor had made most of the decisions; consequently, it didn't allow the managers to grow. They would soon learn that I didn't operate that way.

When problems were presented, my first response was always, "What do you think we should do?" That forced managers to consider possible solutions rather than just dump problems at my doorstep. I told each manager that I respected their judgment and their opinions and that pleased them. If they made a mistake, well, that was part of the learning experience, and hopefully, those mistakes would not reoccur.

When I went on vacation, I told them that I would not be checking in on them as I trusted them to do the right thing. I left by saying, *"Don't call me unless the building is on fire."* That trust built confidence. The result was a dynamic management team and, in turn, productive sales and support staffs. They all made me proud—and they also made me look good!

I See "Big Bob"

Bob Bachmeier

In May of 1994, I drove up to the Twin Cities to visit my parents. While there I decided to stop at Bob Bachmeier's big house overlooking Como Lake. He lived there alone now—the kids were all grown and gone, and he and Lila had also divorced. I didn't know what kind of reception that I would get now that Susie and I were no longer married. I knocked. He answered, and after an awkward moment, he smiled and invited me in. We sat at his kitchen table, drank some whiskey, smoked a few cigarettes, and talked for over an hour. Through the years I had actually grown to like Bob, and I think the feeling was mutual. Six months after that visit, he died of a heart attack at age seventy-two. I attended his visitation and funeral. We had been through a lot, and I was going to miss him.

I Do

In June 1994, Robyn and I were married in a small chapel in Hoover, Alabama. Only a few friends; coworkers; Robyn's parents and her children, Jeremy (eleven) and Jamie (eight), attended. Her parents had never even met me before, and here I was marrying their daughter and whisking her and two of their grandchildren off to Omaha, Nebraska. Where on earth was Omaha? Better yet, where on earth was Nebraska?

We had planned a luncheon afterwards at The Club—a large members-only restaurant on Red Mountain overlooking downtown Birmingham. Her parents announced that they would not be attending the luncheon. Her father had a previous commitment…with the Rotary Club. Their decision not to celebrate Robyn's wedding day had to hurt her immensely, but she refused to show it. Those who did attend enjoyed a wonderful meal, and there were several champagne toasts to celebrate our marriage.

After a quick honeymoon at the Victoria B & B in Anniston (now the Hotel Finial), we packed up the car, loaded in the kids and Sassy (their little dog), and headed for the "heartland" to start our new lives together.

Settling In

For me, it was a new city, a new job, a new house, a new wife, and new kids. All of that most certainly added to my stress level, but at least I had grown up in the Midwest. It wasn't like I had moved to a strange land. But for Robyn, on the other hand, she had walked away from nearly everything familiar—all the customs she had taken for granted her whole life. The move from Alabama to Nebraska was going to be challenging. All she had to do was open her mouth, and that southern drawl would elicit, "Where are you from?" *(I suggested she say SOUTH Omaha).* Sweet tea was not the beverage of choice, and if you ordered a Coke, you weren't asked, "What flavor?" You had to order a glass of POP for that to happen. And other than Cracker Barrel, it was really difficult to find grits. I hated grits.

Like the South, most people were nice, but unlike the South, they didn't drop everything just to have a chat. The pace was just a little quicker, and maybe a little less folksy. Conversations in Omaha were rarely sprinkled with phrases such as "fixin' to," "bless his heart," or "mom'n'em" (*refers to the whole family, not just mom*). She had also left behind her job, her home, her parents and brother, numerous other relatives, schoolmates, friends, plus her southern culture and familiarity—and warmer weather.

We eventually settled into our new home and routines. We, as a family, attended Sunday services at St. Andrew's Methodist church in the auditorium of Millard North High School. The congregation grew, and soon a new church was constructed at 150th and Maple. I was busy with my new job, and Robyn began searching for employment. Jamie and Jeremy were in school (*the top school district in the entire state*), and things seemed to be going well on that front. They appeared to be adjusting, but obviously missed their dad, grandparents, and friends. I suggested that for the first year, we send them back to Birmingham for monthly visits. They would fly out Friday morning and return Sunday afternoon. Initially, it was a little scary putting two unaccompanied kids on an airplane, but the flight attendants watched out for them. They eventually became seasoned airline veterans.

The Collection

On the following few pages are articles that appeared in the Omaha World-Herald's monthly newsletter "Square Talk." That name was derived from the block that the newspaper building occupied... *World-Herald Square.*

I wrote both articles pertaining to my growing newspaper memorabilia collection. I think you'll find that both stories are self-explanatory.

The Golden Rule: MORE and MORE and MORE

Hobby, or Obsession?

Advertising Director Tom Golden with a few pieces from his newspaper memorabilia collection

It was back in 1989 that I became associated with Frank McGinty. I was working at the Saint Paul Pioneer Press at the time and Frank had just joined the saintly city paper after a long and illustrious career at the rival daily, the Minneapolis Star-Tribune. Settling into his new surroundings he displayed a few newspaper carrier and "hawker" figurines in his office. They caught my eye.

Frank noted my curiosity and proudly told me that he had quite a few more newspaper figurines at home. "Really? How interesting." My intrigue in his unusual collection prompted him to bring one of his "duplicates" to me the next day as a present. I was hooked!

I began browsing through gift shops as well as collector and antique stores in search of such figurines. My modest collection grew as I expanded from simply carriers and hawkers to any figurine that included a newspaper. As I traveled to conferences or somewhere on vacation, I began seeking out antique malls and gift shops in every city in hopes of discovering more treasures. MORE is the operative word here.

I got on a number of brochure and catalog mailing lists, subscribed to collector magazines and then decided to expand my horizons by incorporating newspaper-related art, pictures and posters into my growing collection. And as it grew, so did my needs for displaying it.

Upon moving to Omaha in 1994, I made sure that I bought a home large enough for me to use a "spare" bedroom as my very own personal museum gallery. But, I certainly had room for MORE. Then my wife asked what she should do with all this stuff when I died. (Was she planning to kill me?). "Who cares—help me haul this new display case upstairs."

GOLDEN RULES…Newspaper memorabilia collector Tom Golden, OWH advertising director, stands proudly in front of his growing collection of newspaper-related figurines. And, there's room for MORE.

MORE is good, I'd keep telling myself. Cheap ones. Expensive ones. Old ones. New ones. Big ones. Small ones. Quality is all well and good, but the key here is MORE. My collection now numbers 216 pieces—but MORE are coming. Oops, make that 217.

I proudly drag unsuspecting visitors to our home upstairs to see my collection. Reactions vary. Stunned silence is certainly among them. Who cares. Different strokes for different folks. MORE. Maybe a room addition is in order!

Thanks Mr. McGinty, wherever you are (I think I know where my wife wishes you were). Okay boys, that curio cabinet goes right up those stairs.

Square Talk thanks Tom Golden, OWH Advertising Director, for contributing this article (December 1997) which appeared in the Newspaper Memorabilia Collectors Newsletter.

The Golden Rule: There's Still MORE Out There, I Think

Hobby Obsession + Advancing Years = Total Confusion

You'd just better believe Advertising Director Tom Golden knows his own newspaper memorabilia collection, and he's willing to bet on it—especially with his wife.

Sometime back I wrote an article about how my modest collection of newspaper-related figurines had grown into a full-blown obsession. The fact that I'm approaching 250 individual pieces is certainly testimony to that fact. Yes, it's true, I've spent (invested? squandered?) hundreds, nay, thousands on these little men, women, boys, girls, cats, dogs, raccoons, mice, foxes, bees, pigs, rabbits, bears and one lone elephant.

Why?

Because for some reason I feel compelled to buy anything that is clutching a newspaper in some fashion or another. Thank goodness that my REAL newspaper carrier boy has enough sense to peddle by my house at a relatively high rate of speed while flinging my daily paper in the general direction of my driveway. If he happened to wander too close he might end up standing in a corner of my "museum" hollering "EXTRA, EXTRA—Newsboy kidnapped".

Anyway, some of the figurines are cute (can a guy use that word?), some are funny, some are downright clever while others are even thought-provoking. But, one thing you may not realize about having a collection such as this is the incredible amount of dust that it collects.

Now I suppose that I should dust them, but then I'd just have to do it all over again next year—so what's the point? And, after all, this hobby is supposed to be fun—not work.

So, I did the only sensible thing a guy can do under the circumstances... I asked my wife to dust them. (I had no idea that she even knew words like that!). Anyway, apparently, they will remain dusty while I continue my never-ending quest for MORE. *(Point of clarification: my quest is for more figurines, not more dust).*

You may be asking yourself: *"This is all well and good, Tom, but are you ever going to get to the confusion part as promised in the headline?"* Well, yes, I am. Eventually. I'm setting the stage here.

So anyway, my wife, the non-figurine duster with the X-rated mouth (vocabulary?) is frequently amused by all of the little notes I write to myself and unload from my shirt pocket every night after work. You know, reminder notes such as "repair car—passenger door missing" or "7:30 breakfast meeting with Pope at Shoney's".

She seems to think that this is an indication that my memory is slipping. HA. It's actually an indication that I'm losing my mind. But, why quibble over little things.

"Yes, Yes, but is the confusion part ever coming?" Why, yes, it is. Let me now connect the dots.

So, the "dust-free queen" and I were in Birmingham, AL. over the Christmas holidays visiting relatives and other southern-type people when I decided to venture out to prowl for more figurines. I found one in a collector shop and proudly brought it back to the in-law's place to show it off. (They think I'm a crazy Yankee anyway, so no additional harm was anticipated). My wife (now known as Ms. Dusty) quips: *"You've already got that one".*

"DO NOT" I retort defensively and a tad indignantly. *"Yes, you do. I'll bet you fifty dollars".* No time to back down now. There are witnesses *"Oh yeah? I think I know what is in my own collection".*

"REALLY?" she says without hesitation. *"Then it's a bet".*

Oh geez, now my in-laws are looking at me and I'm beginning to flush. I hate that. So, I counter: *"Why to infer that I don't even know my own collection is preposterous. Why, why it's ludicrous. It's ah, goofy. Of course, it's a bet".*

There. Pride still intact. I guess I showed her.

Upon our return home to Omaha, it was a foot race to get to my newspaper shrine room. *I think "Here you go honey—45 - 46"* you may now understand, *"47 - 48"* the confusion part *"49 - 50"*. She couldn't wait to call her folks!

Thanks to World-Herald Advertising Director Tom Golden for contributing his second article to Square Talk (April 1998) on collecting newspaper memorabilia. In his first article, we learned of his rapidly expanding collection, enveloping all available space in his home. In the second installment, we learn how a true collector can easily get in trouble with his wife and in-laws, just trying to keep track of his prized possessions in the never-ending search for MORE.

Minnesota

When the kids headed to Birmingham, Robyn and I would occasionally make the six-hour drive from Omaha to St. Paul to visit my parents and my oldest son, Mike, and his family. If we left on a Friday afternoon for just a quick weekend trip, we'd often spend the night at the Country Inn and Suites in Urbandale, which is just West of Des Moines. On our very first stay there, we discovered that just behind the hotel was an old village re-creation (*now gone*). Historic old buildings from around the area had been moved there to re-create a turn-of-the-century Iowa town. It included several homes, a general store, post office, newspaper building, and a white church with a tall steeple. One beautiful afternoon, we walked hand in hand investigating each of the buildings. We were so head over heels in love that little things brought us such joy.

We usually had dinner at an old-fashioned, dimly lit, and romantic steak house just a few miles from the Country Inn. Breakfast was always at the Machine Shed, which was located right next to the hotel. After breakfast we'd continue our drive up to St. Paul, usually arriving around noon (unless she insisted on stopping at the Medford Outlet Mall).

On more extended trips, we would stay in the Twin Cities for four or five days. Robyn always loved The St. Paul Hotel in downtown St. Paul; but me, being a cheap skate (*a trait I'd learned from Dollar Bill*), I'd always insist that we stay at less expensive places. *Yeah, another regret.* We were, however, staying at the St. Paul Hotel the night that Princess Diana was killed. After we checked in and had eaten dinner, Robyn wanted to stay in the room, cuddle up in the bed, and watch TV. I, on the other hand, wanted to walk around downtown and look at all of the custom and collectible cars that were parked everywhere as part of a big auto show. She stayed—I went. (*Wow, the regrets just keep piling up*). When I finally got back to the room, the news about the deadly crash in Paris was just being broadcast.

On those "extended" trips, we had time to visit points of interest and I loved giving Robyn tours of the area. On one such excursion, we happened to be driving by Snail Lake in Shoreview. She said, "Is that lake frozen solid?" I said yes, it was frozen, but not solid. I

205

presumed it had a foot or more of ice on the surface. I told her that all the lakes in Minnesota were usually frozen this time of year. She then asked if it was safe to walk on. I assured her that it would not only hold people, but also a Winnebago Motor Home. "Can we stop so I walk on it?" she asked. I pulled into the beach parking lot.

Robyn, Sassy and me in 1997

Down at the shoreline she cautiously stepped out just a couple of feet as if testing the surface. She stopped, looked down at the ice, and, then feeling it was safe, ventured out a little further. Then she started laughing and sliding around. It was her first time walking on water...and she was having so much fun doing so. Once again, I couldn't help but notice how she was filled with wonder and joy by such common Midwestern winter things—much like seeing that first snowfall in Omaha. All old stuff for me, but brand-new for her.

The Job and Stock

The ad division was doing very well under the leadership of a strong management team and a results-oriented sales force. We regularly exceeded our annual revenue growth goals and achieved most other division objectives. I frequently got congratulatory notes from the publisher and had received excellent annual salary increases, large stock options, and bonuses. Things were going well, but I continued to be troubled not knowing the results of that telephone "test." I thought if there had been any initial reluctance to hire me, it was due to those test results. I sought and received permission to review them, and as expected, they were not particularly good. There were a lot of mid-range scores with only a few areas in the high-range. I found that annoying but predictable. Thank goodness they had not relied solely on them to make a hiring decision.

Only full-time *Omaha World-Herald* employees could purchase stock in the company. It had averaged a 20 percent value increase annually for thirty years...plus paid dividends. The Omaha Bank (later to become part of US Bank) decided that it was a pretty safe bet to loan newspaper employee's money to purchase shares. The bank held the stock, and as it rose in value, they eventually had enough collateral to loan you up to 100 percent of the cost to buy more shares. As promised, the publisher decided the maximum quantity any individual could buy annually and that usually meant the more important your position, the more shares you were allowed to buy. One big provision: if you left the company for any reason, you were required to sell all your shares back to the company at the current per share price. While there is always risk involved in purchasing stock, based on its thirty-year track record, it sure seemed that this was a good way to make some money. I purchased all that was allocated by the publisher. That was a very smart thing to do.

Our Lives Changed

In the spring of 1998, Robyn was on the phone discussing the kids' summer visit plans to Birmingham with Jerry, her ex. We had decided to send them down for two weeks, but he insisted that they stay for a month. The kids were now so entrenched in Omaha that neither of them wanted to go for an extended period of time. They even argued with us about it…but we reluctantly gave in to Jerry's request.

Shortly after arriving in Birmingham, they were whisked off to a Bible camp, where a friend of Jerry's (I think he was a minister) told them that they should move back to Birmingham and live with their dad and his new wife. In fact, he had personally talked to God about it and was told from on high that "IT WAS GOD'S WILL." Jeremy had a girlfriend back in Omaha, so God's will or not, he wasn't moving. Jamie, on the other hand, was more susceptible to "God's command," and she told us that she wanted to live with her dad. Now twelve, we realized that a court would probably allow her to decide with which parent to live. Robyn and I made a horrible decision in not fighting to keep her in Omaha. We allowed her to move back to Birmingham. *Add that to my ever-growing list of regrets. Probably my biggest.*

Robyn was so distraught that she'd lock herself in the bathroom, and I could hear her sobbing. It just broke my heart. She was so depressed and heartbroken at losing her daughter that, unbeknown to me, had hired a divorce attorney. She planned to move to Birmingham. While I was away at work, she gathered all the financial records requested by her lawyers. Then, in the spring of 1999, when Jeremy got out of school, I was presented with divorce papers. They packed their clothes and drove to Alabama. She rented an apartment in Trussville, where she could be close to her parents and to Jamie. Jeremy alternated staying with her, his dad, and his grandparents. I kept supplying the money Robyn needed to furnish her one-bedroom unit. We occasionally talked on the phone, but we did not see one another over the next few months. I found it curious that she had not signed off on the divorce, and that gave me a glimmer of hope.

Running vs. Smoking

Occasionally, a newspaper vendor or national rep would come to town and want to take me, and a couple members of my management team, out for drinks and dinner. There was always somebody in the group that smoked. I had been off cigarettes and been jogging for sixteen years, but I was totally depressed, and after a drink or two, that pack lying on the table got very tempting. One evening I found myself asking, "Can I bum one of those?" I knew I could smoke one and still not go back—after all, I had will power. Any of you that have ever smoked and quit, can see the quicksand that I was stepping into. One cigarette tends to lead to another. At some point, you begin to feel like a mooch, so you buy a pack. You promise yourself that you'll only smoke them on special social occasions, but that pledge is quickly broken. Eventually, the running stopped and the puffing began in earnest.

A Fateful Conference

It just so happened that I had a Midwest Newspaper Advertising Executives Association conference in Huntsville, Alabama, that September. I called Robyn and told her about the meeting and suggested I fly into Birmingham a few days prior to the conference. I'd make motel and rental car reservations, and after visiting her, I'd drive up to Huntsville. To my surprise and delight, she agreed. The plan was to drop by her apartment for a glass of wine and then go out for dinner. I drove over to Trussville early to locate her apartment building and then decided to drive up the road to a large grocery store to purchase some flowers. As I pulled in, there she was—getting out of her car and heading into that very store. I didn't want our first face-to-face encounter in months to be inside a grocery store or out in a parking lot, so I waited until she returned to her car and drove out. I bought the flowers, and then nervously drove over to her apartment. I wondered how things would go: Would I get a cold greeting, or would the flowers earn me one that was lukewarm? WOW… I never expected a HOT reception.

I knocked on her door, and when she answered, we just looked at each other…then embraced. I told her how much I still loved her and missed her. She said that she had missed me and loved me as well and that leaving me had been a huge mistake. She said that she had come to realize that her place was with me and that was why she had not signed the divorce papers. I cancelled the motel room, returned the rental car, and stayed with her. Two days later we packed up her car and were on our way to Huntsville. She was coming back home—to Omaha. Jeremy would fly up to join us in a week.

The conference was at that Marriott Hotel located adjacent to the US Space and Rocket Museum. I checked-in while Robyn waited in the car with Sassy. Dogs were not allowed in the hotel, so I was going to have to smuggle her in. While Robyn went up to the room, I put the dog in a duffle bag and casually walked through the lobby and into an open elevator. Oh great, it was filled with fellow conference attendees and spouses. Someone remarked that my bag appeared to be moving, so I unzipped the top and a little head popped out. Cutest thing you ever saw. They wanted me to bring Sassy into the hospitality suite, but that would be dangerous as hotel employees were in and out. So she stayed quietly in our room.

After the conference, we were approaching Nashville on the trip back to Omaha when Robyn said, "Would you mind making a detour?" She had briefly attended Tennessee Tech with her first husband, Mike Vise. They had gotten married right out of high school, and he had received a football scholarship at the school. I said, "Sure," but was surprised that she wanted to go back to Cookeville. You see, Mike was killed in an automobile accident while driving through Nashville on his way home to Birmingham to visit his parents. Robyn had stayed behind at their campus apartment. I never asked why he went alone. It was obviously a very painful memory, and besides, it was none of my business.

After that tragedy she moved back to Birmingham and stayed with her parents. They were naturally overly-protective of their little girl and consequently tended to smother her. Wanting to regain some independence, she eventually moved into an apartment complex where she met a neighbor—Jerry Turner. Long story short, they married and had two children—Jeremy and Jamie.

So in case you were counting, yes, I was Robyn's third husband.

When we reached Cookeville, she gave me directions and we drove around the college campus. We then pulled into the parking lot just outside of the apartment that she and Mike had shared. I knew better than to utter a single word. I could see that she was re-living events that had occurred in that building as tears streamed down her face. I can't even begin to imagine the pain that she suffered upon learning of his death. It was such a traumatic event, and both of them were so young—just kids. She finally whispered, "Okay, we can go." We drove west on Interstate 40 in complete silence.

New-New-New

Once back in Omaha, we decided that we'd like to have a fresh start by buying a new house. After all, this was MY house, not OUR house.

We loved looking through various subdivisions and especially going to open houses. One Sunday we were driving through Huntington Park, a subdivision in West Omaha out by 156th and Blondo, when a home under construction caught our eye. It was a big two-story house with four bedrooms, three and half baths, a three-car garage, and "Graceland" pillars flanking the front door. The rooms were all framed, the electrical wiring complete, and the plumbing roughed in, but no sheetrock had been hung. We could choose our own flooring, fixtures, lighting, cabinetry, trim, appliances, colors, etc. and that sounded like great fun. So we bought all those things always exceeding the builder's "allowance." Then I got carried away with upgrades. Even Robyn tried to rein me in, but I was on an expensive roll. The builder fell in love with me and my constant pricey change orders. When all was said and done, we (okay, mostly I) had added over $50,000 to the original $300,000 purchase price. But it sure turned out beautiful.

2628 North 160th Ave., Huntington Park, Omaha, NE

Well, you can't have a new house without new furniture. We got a credit card at Nebraska Furniture Mart and used the hell out of it. Then I pondered, *Could you park old cars in a new garage?* I didn't think so. Robyn got a new VW Passat, and I got a new Jeep Grand Cherokee. As you can well imagine, our debt load was skyrocketing. I cashed in the 401K that remained at the *Birmingham News* and was hit with a nasty penalty, but we needed the money.

I suggested to Robyn that we keep the apartment in Trussville so that she could visit her daughter and parents whenever she wanted, but she flatly refused to even consider it. The apartment contents were shipped to Omaha and stored in the new home's three-car garage (much to the dismay of the builder). We quickly sold the Lloyd Street house and moved into our new home. We finally had a place that we picked out TOGETHER. We sure were happy—but happiness is a fleeting thing.

Robyn's Parents

Despite a rather rocky start, I now got along just famously with Bob and Ellen, Robyn's parents. Her dad was such a nice, soft-spoken, gentle man…and so generous. As an example, when we'd go to Birmingham, we'd always get the use of their big pearl white Cadillac. Bob *(Can you believe it…another Bob)* was a funeral director, and he also had another vehicle to use—a black Buick, which was his company car. One day, Robyn and I had been out all day in the Caddy and returned to her parents' house about four o'clock in the afternoon. We were all going out later for dinner (Daddy, of course, would always insist on paying). I was inside with Robyn and her mother and just happened to look out the window. There was Bob, cleaning the car's windshield with Windex and paper towels. Then he and the car disappeared. While we were in the kitchen drinking wine, he was out filling up the gas tank for us.

Whenever we all went out to dinner, I was always the "designated driver." Bob would ride shotgun sipping on a screwdriver while Robyn and Ellen rode in back enjoying some chardonnay. We'd frequently go the Bright Star in Bessemer. It was a long drive from Trussville, but they served great food in a wonderful old-world atmosphere.

Robyn and I once drove down to Kansas City to meet up with her parents who were there attending a funeral director's conference. That Friday evening we had cocktails in their Crowne Center hotel room, and then went out to a nearby steak house for dinner. On Saturday, it was suggested that we squeeze in a trip to one of the local casinos. Whenever we got together, we always had a good time. I had been accepted into the Nolen family and was so happy to be a part of it.

One summer, Robyn and I were vacationing in Orange Beach, Alabama. *(Destin, Ft. Walton, Orange beach, etc. are all a part of the "Redneck Riviera".)* Coincidentally, her parents were attending yet another funeral director's conference at the swanky Grand Hotel Point Clear near Mobile. Their meetings were sure held at nice places! Anyway, Robyn and I drove over to meet with them for dinner in that elegant resort dining room. Coats were required for men, and thankfully, Bob had an extra sport coat that I could wear.

When we arrived that afternoon, the big circular driveway at the hotel's front entrance was lined with brand-new hearses. We knew why they were there (vendors), but newly arriving guests sure wouldn't. Guest: *"What's with all the hearses?"* Front desk clerk: *"Food poisoning. Will you be dining with us this evening?"* That's a joke. I'm not really suggesting that the Grand Hotel has ever poisoned its guests. Lawyers are so picky!

I'm Dyeing Up Here

Because I was more than a little self-conscience about being eleven years older than Robyn, I always tried to look a bit younger by hiding my gray. Every six weeks or so my barber would color my hair my natural color, well, okay, my ONCE natural color, a medium shade of brown. On one such visit, after my haircut but before my coloring, I just happened to mention that the prior job had turned out just a little light. It was more like a dark blond. He said he had probably washed it a bit too soon and we'd try leaving the color in just a little longer this time. So, as I recall the events of the day, he proceeded to apply semi-permanent color to my hair, permanent color to my eyebrows, and then set the timer.

As I was the only customer in the shop, he decided to make some calls to his regulars to remind them it was time to come in. He'd then schedule their appointments. Very proactive. Well, in between those calls, the phone rang and it was his teenage daughter. They got into a lengthy conversation and neither of us noticed that the timer had gone off. Once he finally hung up, he said to me, "Let's go wash it." So over to the sink we went. He washed it—**TWICE**. I noticed as he did so that he kept scrubbing my ears, forehead, and the back of my neck. He then toweled it off, and as we walked back over to the barber chair, I glanced in the mirror… AND PANICKED. "That looks awfully dark, Mike," I managed to utter. "Well, it's still wet. Let me blow dry it and see if it lightens up a bit." It didn't. He finally spun me around so I could look into the large mirror on the wall. Instead of my hair being a medium shade of brown, it and my eyebrows were JET BLACK. To add to the misery, there were also black smudges on my ears, forehead, and neck. "Wash it often—it should lighten up," he said. Great.

I walked slowly down Dodge Street towards the World-Herald building with my head hung low. I knew people wouldn't giggle in my face because I was the boss…but behind my back, there would be howls of laughter. How embarrassing. As I rushed through the front lobby, I could feel the stares of the front counter staffers. I made my way up to the advertising division and into my office. Well, the entire front wall of my office consisted of glass, and it wasn't long before people began wandering by and looking in. It hadn't taken long for word to spread. I was now the side show.

It just so happened that Robyn was going to pick me up in front of the building that evening so we could go out to dinner. I stood on the sidewalk waiting for her to pull up. When she did, I opened the passenger door and started to climb in. That's when I heard her uncontrollable laughter. She finally re-gained enough control to say, "Oh my God, you look like Groucho Marx."

Here We Go Again

It was the fall of 2000, and we had been living in our beautiful Huntington Park home for six or seven months. The house had been decorated with the help of an interior designer, and it was gorgeous. Robyn had invited her parents to visit, and she was so excited about seeing them and having them see her lovely new home. It was a wonderful visit, and as usual, we had such a great time together. I would only get to see them one more time—that upcoming Christmas.

In November and December, Robyn started slipping back into her funk. She was visibly unhappy again but refused to discuss it. Once again, she was pulling away from me. One evening we were out having dinner and discussing our upcoming holiday trip to Birmingham. For seven years we had always taken an early flight out of Omaha, through Memphis, and into Birmingham around 10:00 a.m. When I mentioned that flight for our upcoming trip, she became unglued. "I hate that flight," she snapped. *Really?* I thought. *And it took seven years to mention it?* But that kind of behavior was becoming typical as she became increasingly distant. She got upset about little things but would never want to talk about them. I often got the silent treatment and couldn't figure out why. Now look, I'm no angel. I'm sure that she had good cause to be upset with me at times. I could be insensitive, get angry, be somewhat controlling, and maybe even manipulative. I apologized for whatever it was that I had done to upset her—but to no avail.

When we flew down to Birmingham to celebrate Christmas with her family, I could tell she was depressed and she was hardly talking to me. She went off with her mother and her daughter shopping leaving me behind with nothing to do. I cruised around town aimlessly in the big white caddy—and was so bored that I stopped to bowl a couple of games by myself. The silent treatment continued, and things between us worsened.

Such a Sad Ending

The trip was over, and we were back in Omaha. Unbeknown to me, she was once again meeting with the divorce lawyers. She handed me the papers in March. That is when she moved most of her things out of the master bedroom and into the guest bedroom. In late April she asked me to move out. I pleaded with her, but she had made up her mind. She told me that if I refused to go that she would get a court order.

I rented a furnished apartment while continuing to maintain the yard and pay all the bills. I wanted to reconcile. NO. I wanted a trial separation. NO. I offered to rent her an apartment in Birmingham so that she could visit as often as she wished. NO. She was demanding a divorce, and that for me was like getting stabbed in the heart.

Lawyers are expensive, so I put together what I considered to be a fair settlement offer. She had come into our marriage with virtually nothing except a lot of credit card debt. I had paid all that off for her. My financial proposal called for us to split everything 50-50 since our marriage in June 1994. She was very reluctant to deal directly with me as she apparently thought that I was trying to cheat her. I wasn't. As expected, her lawyers balked at everything. My lawyer advised me to stop communicating with her entirely. I just couldn't do that.

One evening I went over to pick up mail and discuss a feasible settlement. She was so frazzled. She argued with me about everything until I yelled, "Robyn, what the hell do you want?" With that, she said, "Please don't yell at me," as she backed up against the kitchen cabinets, then slowly slid down them until she was sitting on the floor. She put her hands up to her face and sobbed, "I just want to go home." She was so frustrated, and I felt so horrible. I apologized and left. I still loved her so much.

I was driving back to my apartment when I decided to call her to be sure she was all right. I again told her that I was sorry for shouting, then asked, "What can I do?" She said, "If you make my next month's car payment, pay my attorney's fees, and pay for my moving expenses, I'll accept the offer that you brought over tonight." I typed up a new agreement outlining the property and cash settlement and included her latest requests. We mutually agreed to it, and we both signed. This annoyed the hell out of our attorneys: Her lawyers claimed they could get her more; my attorney argued that I was giving way too much. It's possible both were upset because the meters were about to stop running. *(Okay, I'm a little jaded. My apology to all divorce lawyers out there.)*

On Sunday, September 3, 2001, almost exactly two years after she had said to me, *"Leaving you was such a mistake—I now know that I belong with you"* …she was gone, and this time it was forever.

On Thursday, November 1, 2001, I was to appear in court. My lawyer told me that the judge would ask if I wanted the divorce. I told her that I didn't and that I'd have to say no. She advised that I not do that or the divorce would drag on for months. Robyn did not appear, but her attorney indicated that she wanted the divorce. As predicted, the judge asked me if I also wanted it. I sat in silence, then with tears rolling down my cheeks whispered, "Yes." It was painfully obvious to the judge and to everyone else that I did not want the divorce, but I had said yes, so the dissolution was officially granted.

I honestly didn't know that a human being could cry as hard, and as often, as I did that first year. I literally broke down daily—sometimes before I left for work, sometimes when I returned home after work. On many days it was BOTH. I actually had to see my doctor four times during that period because I continued to get sinus infections. I wasn't just brokenhearted, I was totally devastated. I no longer cared much about anything and feared what I might do if the deep depression continued.

I tried to hide my misery from my co-workers. I smiled and cracked jokes like the "old Tom," but I'm sure that they noticed my puffy bloodshot eyes. Maybe they thought that I had developed a drinking problem. I hadn't. My life was so empty without her.

An Expensive Diversion

Rather than kill myself, I decided to concentrate on my new hobby… GAMBLING.

Having nobody to go home to, I spent a lot of time at all three casinos in Council Bluffs, Iowa (just across the river from downtown Omaha): Harvey's, Ameristar, and Bluff's Run. I was not into poker, blackjack, roulette or craps… I was into slot machines. I played mostly dollar slots—two and three coins at a time.

Machines back then accepted paper money, or they could be hand fed with a specific coin denomination. They paid out, however, only in coins. If you hit something good, coins would pour out into the tray. The problem was that the machines frequently ran out of money, so you'd have to stand and wait until a slot attendant came over with a bag (or bags) of coins to refill it. There were multiple types of coins that only worked in a machine of the same denomination (penny coins in a penny machine, quarter coins in a quarter machine, dollar coins in the dollar machines, etc.). You carried a plastic bucket around with you to hold your coins.

Not only were the machines coin operated, they were also a lot looser than they are now. They even had slot machine "odds" posted by the cashier's window. I watched as they gradually slid from the mid-90s (percent) into the high-80s (percent). I have no idea where they are today. But before the odds sank, I actually hit a number of *"jackpots"* ranging from $1,200 to $12,500.

*$10,000 slot machine jackpot at Ameristar in
Council Bluffs, IA. (June 27, 2002)*

Let me explain: a taxable *"jackpot"* is one whereby you hit $1,200 or more on a single spin—not the cumulative total on the machine resulting from multiple spins. If a machine hit $1,199 on a single spin, it was NOT a taxable jackpot. But add that extra dollar, making it $1,200, and the machine locked up, a flashing red light on the top turned on, and loud music would begin playing (usually "I'm in the money").

A jackpot required a "hand pay" as well as the signing of a 1099 tax form. You had to declare these $1,200 plus winnings as income or have proof of off-setting gambling losses. Because I always inserted my casino membership card into the machines prior to playing, the casino kept track of all my winnings and losses should I need them for the IRS.

One year I had $82,000 in jackpot earnings and all of it was offset with losses. Is it any wonder that the casinos lavished me with private club memberships, meals, hotel rooms, cocktails, trips, merchandise, and gambling incentives? I had the "TOP TEIR" card at all three Council Bluff casinos. I knew that if I kept this up I'd probably go broke. I began giving serious consideration to finding a new hobby.

Chardonnay... Not Just for Drinking:

In May 2003, I bought a little six-week-old puppy, one of five in the litter, from a woman who worked in our classified advertising department. The little white fur ball, half bichon and half toy poodle, had been born on St. Patrick's Day; and she weighed next to nothing. Besides being lovable and cute beyond belief, she didn't shed. *JACKPOT!*

I asked my management team for name suggestions and got names such as Snowball, White-Out, and Cocaine. I feared that if I used that last one, when I called her, *"COCAINE, here, COCAINE,"* either the police would show up or I'd be mobbed by a bunch of drug addicts. I chose the name *Chardonnay.*

When I brought her home, she refused to eat. I had no idea what to do but thought, *Well, she's a baby, so let's try some baby food.* I went down to the store, picked up some Gerber's, warmed it up in the microwave, and then spoon fed it to her. I hoped I wouldn't have to do that the rest of her, or my, life.

Housebreaking her turned out to be a serious challenge. I was beginning to think that maybe I had bought a "cute" breed, but possibly not a "smart" breed. Eventually, she figured it out. I'd read all about crate training but decided to allow her to sleep in bed with me. I found it interesting that she felt the most comfortable wrapped around the top of my head.

As I was still working, I purchased a children's safety gate and blocked off the laundry room doorway each morning. That room had a vinyl floor, so if she had to go, the cleanup would be easy. She may have been smarter than I had given her credit for as I'd frequently come home to an empty laundry room. She was a heck of a good climber.

I took her everywhere with me including places like Target, Home Depot, PetSmart, and a local landscape nursery. As it was summer, I usually had my driver's side car window down and I'd hold her with my left arm while steering with my right. That allowed her to stick her head out the window, which I knew dogs loved.

My sweet little "Chardonnay". Born March 17, 2003 and died November 16, 2017.

One day I was headed to Target and had just backed out of my driveway. I put the car in Drive and slowly started moving forward. I doubt that I had even reached ten miles per hour when she jumped out the window. It was quite the drop from the Jeep Grand Cherokee. To say the least, I was stunned. I'd never heard of a dog doing that. She landed well away from the car and rolled at least once. I slammed on the brakes and came to a complete stop as she got back up on all fours. She just stood there looking up at me like it was my fault. I guess maybe it was. Thankfully, she hadn't been hurt.

In yet another rare "discovery" moment, I was walking her near the boat launch at White Bear Lake in the Twin Cities. I had never taken her down to the water's edge before, and I did so just to see if she'd get her paws wet. Well, she had no concept of water. To her it was just another surface to run on. She ran full tilt into the lake until the water was up to her neck. She turned and gave me that surprised and accusing look. The same one I got when she jumped out the car window. Once again—my fault.

What a little sweetheart.

-30-
(A term used by journalists to indicate the end of a story)

At age fifty-nine and a half, I decided to retire from the *Omaha World-Herald* and the newspaper industry. A very large competitor called the Internet was looming on the horizon. I knew that it would eventually eat all our classified advertising, which represented nearly half of our total ad revenues. I had put up valiant battles against other media competitors for thirty-nine years, but I just didn't feel up to another one.

Me and sons Mike, Bob, and Tom Jr. at my Omaha World-Herald retirement dinner at the Omaha Country Club on November 8, 2004.

At the end of 2004, Chardonnay and I moved to Nashville: *Music City. The Ryman Auditorium. The Grand Ole Opry. Honky-tonks. Music Row. The Country Music Hall of Fame. Pedal-bars!*

A January 2013 article in the *New York Times* named Nashville the new "it" city. That article, along with the TV show *Nashville*, are at least partially responsible for the area's population explosion and popularity with tourists from around the world.

I decided to live in Franklin, a city seventeen miles south of downtown Nashville, off I-65. It has beautiful wooded rolling hills; a quaint, historic, and vibrant downtown; cannons everywhere; and is located in Williamson County, which has the best school district in the state. That is VERY important from a real estate re-sale standpoint. So...

I bought a house.

I purchased a convertible and a pool table.

I became a Realtor.

For seven years, I spent one-third of my time in St. Paul caring for my aging parents.

I quit smoking—AGAIN!

I joined the "Y" and lost thirty pounds.

I got cancer.

I wrote a book.

On occasion, I still practice on my old hobby...gambling, but now, I don't have to carry around a coin bucket. Everything is computerized. Unfortunately, the losses continue to offset the winnings... BY A LOT! Someday I'll learn that in the end, the house always wins.

Finally, Susie and I remain friends, all three boys turned out great, we have eight grandchildren, and Robyn has re-married. As for me, let's just say that while time marches on, it doesn't necessarily heal all wounds.

In Grateful Appreciation

Before I finished editing my manuscript, I asked several people to read through the rough drafts. They willingly agreed to do so knowing full well that their draft copy may be riddled with errors. They knew that because I had warned them in advance. A difficult task for them to be sure.

Well, no good deed goes unpunished. Some early draft readers were subjected to incomplete sentences, run-on sentences, redundancy, mis-spellings, missing letters or words, duplicate letters or words, weird, and sometimes bizarre punctuation, incomplete thoughts (well, that's kind of my specialty), scrambled timelines, insufficient explanations, and explanation "overkill." I was even guilty of dangling a few participles…and I don't even know what a participle is.

I did ten drafts/re-writes, and along the way, most manuscript readers offered sage advice and ideas (greatly appreciated). ALL readers offered me encouragement—especially Jerry. After reading my initial draft, which was still pretty rough, his first e-mail to me regarding the book read: "Couldn't stop reading. I found it to be funny, factual and very entertaining…it brought back a lot of memories." His second e-mail read: "I started to read it again and am actually having more fun the second time through. I'm seeing things that I went over too fast or they just didn't sink in. It's pretty good, Tom." Well, that was certainly high praise coming from my big brother. Everyone said, "Publish it," so with some fear and trepidation, I did—mostly for Jerry.

THANK YOU to my early draft readers, including Jerry Golden, Mary Streeter, Barb Kearney, Diana Condon, Bob Rudman, Ted Krammer, Sarah Golden, Collin Brace, and Bob

Golden, and to my later draft readers Susie Bachmeier Golden, Mike Golden, and Robyn Nolen Little.

Thanks also to the Minnesota Historical Society for information on the Shoreview TV tower collapse.

NOTE: *I left a copy of draft 5 for Jerry when I visited him in Florida April 28–May 4, 2018, but he never got a chance to read it. He had been unable to sleep, was extremely tired, and not feeling very well when I saw him. Despite that, he was good-natured and happy-go-lucky as always. He was hardly ever without a BIG smile on his face. We had such a fun week together. He died suddenly on Saturday, May 19, 2018. Oh, how I loved him, and oh, how I miss GO-GEE.*

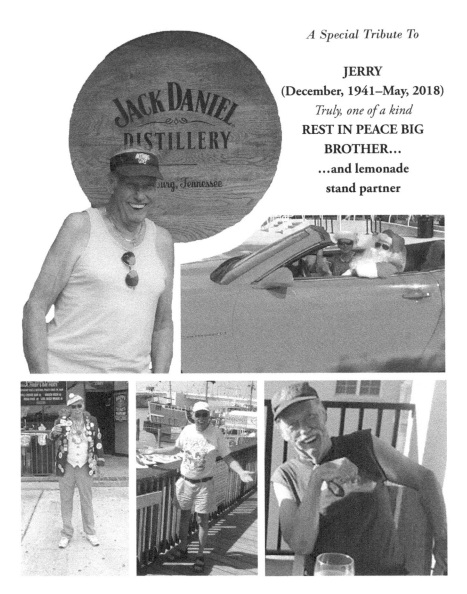

A Special Tribute To

JERRY
(December, 1941–May, 2018)
Truly, one of a kind
REST IN PEACE BIG
BROTHER...
...and lemonade
stand partner

In loving memory:

DAD
Jack Golden (1914–2012)

MOM
Helen Golden (1914–2015)

About the Author

Tom and his older brother, Jerry, were born and raised in St. Paul, Minnesota. He attended and graduated from St. Andrew's Catholic Grade School followed by Cretin High School. St Andrew's was run by the Sisters of Notre Dame and Cretin, a mandatory ROTC program school, was run by the Christian Brothers with some assistance from the US Army. As he puts it, "I was always the kid with the witty comebacks and smart a_ _ remarks, so the nuns whacked my knuckles for eight years and then the Brothers paddled my backside for the next four."

Married at nineteen, Tom worked in the accounting department of several different companies while attending night school at the University of Minnesota. A small want ad in the newspaper changed his career path...and his life.

He spent nearly four decades in the newspaper business. "Nope," he says, "not on the Ivory Tower side, but rather the commercial business side—ADVERTISING and MARKETING." Starting out as a rookie classified advertising outside sales rep with no sales experience, he went on to become the vice president/advertising director for the *St. Paul Pioneer Press*. He was recruited by the *Birmingham* (AL.) *News & Post Herald*, where he was the director of sales and marketing. Again recruited, he left Birmingham for the director of advertising position at the then employee-owned, *Omaha World-Herald*.

Tom decided to take an early retirement at age fifty-nine and a half and move to Franklin, Tennessee (just outside of Nashville). He spends a great deal of his time volunteering for community organizations in Franklin and Williamson County. In between his volunteer work, he wrote this book.